POETRY'S PLAYGROUND

Landscapes of Childhood

POETRY'S PLAYGROUND

The Culture of Contemporary American Children's Poetry

JOSEPH T. THOMAS, JR.

WAYNE STATE UNIVERSITY PRESS
DETROIT

Library of Congress Cataloging-in-Publication Data
Thomas, Joseph T., 1972–
Poetry's playground : the culture of contemporary American children's poetry /
Joseph T. Thomas, Jr.
p. cm. — (Landscapes of childhood)
Includes bibliographical references and index.
ISBN-13: 978-0-8143-3296-2
ISBN-10: 0-8143-3296-X (pbk. : alk. paper)
1. Children's poetry, American—History and criticism. 2. Children—Books and reading—
United States—History—20th century. 3. Children—Books and reading—United States—
History—21st century. 4. American poetry—20th century—History and criticism. 5. American
poetry—21st century—History and criticism. I. Title.
PS310.C5T48 2007
811.009'9282—dc22   2006028490

Please refer to the Permissions Acknowledgments section at the back of this volume
regarding previously printed material.

∞ The paper used in this publication meets the minimum requirements
of the American National Standard for Information Sciences—
Permanence of Paper for Printed Library Materials, ANSI Z39.48-1984.

Designed by Elizabeth Pilon
Typeset by Maya Rhodes
Composed in Berkeley and Middleton

for Terry

Contents

Acknowledgments

First, I would like to thank my colleagues here at California State University, Northridge—particularly Ian Barnard, Kent Baxter, Dorothy Clark, Charles Hatfield, Rick Mitchell, and Jackie Stallcup—for their friendship and encouragement. The intellectual community they have provided has enriched my scholarship and my teaching, making my first few years in Los Angeles a delight. I also thank Elizabeth Say, Gordon Nakagawa, and the administrators of the CSUN Faculty Research and Creative Activity Award and the CSUN College of Humanities Faculty Fellows program for providing me much needed release time. I simply would not have been able to finish this manuscript without it.

I am thankful as well to everyone I have worked with at Wayne State University Press. Annie Martin in particular has made the entire publication process a delight, and I thank her for that. My colleagues, friends, and professors at Illinois State University—both inside and outside of the children's literature program—also deserve a word of thanks. Karen Chachere, Michael Martin, and Christopher McGee, all former classmates at ISU, continue to provide me with an intellectual community without peer. Many of the ideas in this book first took form while talking with them at the Coffee House or over beers at some otherwise forgettable party.

My friend and teacher Jan Susina has offered me many hours of conversation and debate, from which emerged the book you are now holding. He has engaged draft after draft, watching this book grow from a single seminar paper on *The Bat-Poet*, which I prepared for him back in 1998, into my dissertation. For what I've done with it in the years since I left ISU only I am to blame. I hope he approves of the final product.

I also would like to thank Victoria Harris, one of the finest professors I have had the good fortune to work with. Her wit, intelligence, and friendship continue to motivate me. Lissa Paul read and responded to much of this book, particularly the second and third chapters. Her intellectual acumen and enthusiastic support have greatly improved this study. Anita Tarr's suggestions and advice were also a great help. Caroline Jones, whom I've known since our first day of graduate school, has been a constant comfort. Her close and repeated readings of my work have proved invaluable. June Cummins has been a support and an indispensable resource throughout the revision process, as have Philip Nel and Michael Heyman. Thanks also to Willard Bohn, whose productiveness, rigor, and insight is a constant—if somewhat intimidating—inspiration. A consummate scholar, Willard is also one of the most gracious and considerate people I've had the pleasure to meet.

My dear friend Katie E. Strode also deserves a word of thanks for her kindness and love. Her assistance with the appendixes is especially appreciated. Although it was a tedious task, let no one say it was an unappreciated one. Her meticulous reading of the entire book while in manuscript form led to some important last-minute revisions, sharpening some of my fuzzier points.

A special thanks goes to my old friends Steve Halm, J. P. Palmer, and Mason Tromblee for their great encouragement over the years. Additionally, thanks to David Zimmerman, who, besides being a steadfast friend and companion in mischief, opened my eyes to the world of the avant-garde. I thank David, Adam Jones, and Michael Joseph for convincing me that the absurd and trans-rational are not only a source of delight but also a legitimate area of academic study. Thanks also to my friend Tina Rodriguez for reminding me—years before I began this project—of the joys of Shel Silverstein's poetry. I think of her fondly whenever I read his work.

Richard Flynn, my friend and mentor, has aided me with his uncompromising demand for excellence and his unwavering friendship. This book would have been impossible were it not for him and his many suggestions and criticisms. I also thank Eric Nelson, my first and best teacher of poetry. One of my oldest friends, Eric taught me to write. My best prose is attributable to him; my worst, only to me.

I also wish to thank Carmen M. Ganser for her love and patience. Carmen has supported me in this project since its beginning. Thank you for reading and rereading passage after passage of this book in all of its many incarnations. You've not only made it better but you've also made me better. I love you.

The encouragement and love of my family—Joseph Terry Thomas, Sr., Patricia Thomas, and Becky Buddenbaum—inform my every undertaking. You are my oldest friends.

Finally, I must thank Patricia Pace, whose grace and love have impacted me in ways I simply cannot express. Whenever I write, Patti is my true audience. May she rest in peace.

Chapters 2, 3, and segments of chapter 5 appeared, in somewhat different form, in *Children's Literature*, *Children's Literature Association Quarterly*, and *Style*, respectively. Over the years, I have been a regular attendee of Middle Tennessee State University's Modern Critical Approaches to Children's Literature biannual conference, as well as the annual conferences of the American Literature Association and the Children's Literature Association. The ideas for much of this book first took form at these conferences. I thank their organizers and attendees, as well as the editors and peer reviewers of the previously mentioned journals for their feedback. Finally, Arnold Adoff, X. J. Kennedy, and J. Patrick Lewis deserve thanks for the generosity they showed me during the permissions process.

Also thanks to Carrie Downes and Jill Hughes for their help in getting this mass of words into publishable form.

Introduction

This book was originally conceived as a critical history of children's poetry written and published in the United States after the mid-1950s. The scope of that project, however, proved too large for a single book. Although children's poetry has been a part of the field of children's literature since its beginnings, very little critical or historical attention has been paid to the genre, and most of the attention that has been paid concentrates on work produced in Canada and Great Britain. The gap in scholarship at this time is simply too large to be filled by one book. *Poetry's Playground,* then, strives not to be a comprehensive treatment of contemporary U.S. children's poetry. It has the more modest aim of simply broaching the subject.

As this is the first extended foray into relatively uncharted ground, I try to avoid two interrelated problems that are common to most studies of children's poetry. Most critical treatments of children's poetry, particularly U.S. children's poetry, divorce the object of their study from its larger, poetic context. That is, children's poetry is usually treated in isolation, as something wholly apart from the poetic traditions of adult poetry. The second, related problem is that these studies, though they are of high quality, are somewhat insular, referring largely to other studies of children's poetry or, more broadly, to other studies of children's literature, drawing only infrequently on the critical and historical conversations surrounding adult poetic texts. The same problem exists in the world of adult poetry and criticism. When it comes to poetry criticism, stark lines are drawn between the child world and its adult counterpart. This study seeks to dissolve those borders. Even as it maps the uncharted and irregular terrain of U.S. children's poetry, it does so mindful of adult poetry criticism, with the aim of situating children's poetry in the larger context of mid-century and contemporary poetry. An implicit argument throughout this book is that children's poetry is an oft-neglected but nonetheless important part of the poetic tradition of the United States.

The scope of this study is limited historically and geographically to children's poetry written in the United States from around 1959, the publication date of John Ciardi's *The Reason for the Pelican.* The mid-century marks a decisive shift in the market for and attitudes toward U.S. children's poetry, one that corresponds to a much discussed shift in adult poetry. At that time, many U.S. poets who wrote exclusively for adults began also writing for children—poets like Gwendolyn Brooks, John Ciardi, Randall Jarrell (whose children's fiction is peppered with poetry), Sylvia Plath, Theodore Roethke, William Jay Smith, May Swenson, and Richard Wilbur. That these respected poets began to believe that writing for children was an aesthetically rewarding and professionally acceptable enterprise suggests that children's poetry was beginning to be taken seriously as literature in the United States. Although T. S. Eliot, Langston Hughes, Carl Sandburg, and even Gertrude Stein wrote texts for children in the first half of the twentieth century, the end of World War II saw an unprecedented interest in childhood and children's poetry in the United States. The end of the war brought with it plenty of children, and as these children grew, they comprised a huge market for children's texts. As birth rates rose, middle-class Americans found they had more disposable income, and they spent much of it on household goods and the children in those households. As Stephanie Coontz argues in *The Way We Never Were,* the 1950s marked the beginning of the "youth market" and the inception of what would soon become "institutionalized" as "the youth culture" (38).

Although it would be overstating the situation to argue that U.S. poetry was polarized by the much debated "anthology wars" of the late '50s and early '60s, the apparent differences between the two major anthologies of the time, *The New Poets of England and America* (1957) and *The New American Poetry* (1960), reified aesthetic debates of the 1950s and continue to frame most discussions of contemporary poetry. Furthermore, the so-called cult of Frost (Frost wrote the introduction to *The New Poets of England and America*) found themselves invested in writing poetry for children and about childhood, even as Frost himself became what we might call the United States' "official school poet" by the early '60s. X. J. Kennedy, who was featured in Donald Hall and Robert Pack's second selection of *The New Poets of England and America,* would become a strong advocate for and writer of children's poetry, composing essays on the subject and editing with his wife, Dorothy Kennedy, *Knock at a Star* (1982 and 1999) and *Talking Like the Rain* (1992), two popular anthologies of children's poetry. Hall himself would go on to edit his impressive *Oxford Book of Children's Verse in America* in 1985, scaling the project down for children in 1999 with *The Oxford Illustrated Book of American Children's Poems.* The worlds of mainstream American poetry and children's poetry intersect more frequently than is generally assumed.

The more formally experimental poets of the so-called New American line also became increasingly interested in both writing for children and teaching children to write. New York School poets Kenneth Koch and Ron Padgett, for instance, dedicated themselves to poets-in-the-schools programs. Koch, Padgett's teacher at Columbia and one of the principal poets represented in *The New American Poetry*, would write a pair of seminal works concerning teaching children poetry: *Wishes, Lies, and Dreams* (1970) and its companion anthology of poetry by children, *Rose, Where Did You Get That Red?* (1973). Throughout the next two decades these books would provoke much debate on how poetry should be taught to children, with Koch's thesis that children are "natural poets" tackled most strenuously by Myra Cohn Livingston in her two-part essay "But Is It Poetry?" (1976). Livingston would later extend her arguments against Koch in *The Child as Poet: Myth or Reality?* (1984). However, Koch did not limit himself to pedagogical concerns, for in 1985 he would edit, along with Kate Farrell, *Talking to the Sun: An Illustrated Anthology of Poems for Young People*. Again, the history of contemporary American children's poetry is the history of poetry for adults.

Canonical issues frame this book. Chapter 1 traces Robert Frost's emergence as the U.S.'s official school poet, exploring the political and aesthetic dimensions of his canonization and who that canonization pushed to the side. Likewise, the book closes with a look at eight major U.S. anthologies of children's poetry, positing for the sake of future scholarship a list of the most anthologized and best-represented poets of U.S. children's poetry. Frost is certainly among that number.

Chapter 2 concerns Randall Jarrell, another official school poet. Beginning with a reevaluation of the aforementioned "anthology wars," this chapter examines Jarrell's poetics and investigates the implications of a mainstream adult poet who uses a children's book to work through his theoretical notions of poetry. By comparing Jarrell's recently rediscovered essay "Levels and Opposites"—his only surviving extended theoretical discussion of poetics—with *The Bat-Poet* (1964), we see how the poetry and the narrative that surrounds it negotiates and problematizes the binaries suggested by the anthology wars, the "raw" *New American Poetry* (1960) and the "cooked" *New Poets of England and America*. Furthermore, as several of the poems within *The Bat-Poet* also appear in Jarrell's *The Lost World* (1965), his work provides occasion to interrogate the bifurcation of adult and children's literature by writing simultaneously for a child and adult audience.

Chapter 3 addresses poetry actually written and performed by children: the poetry of the playground. Relying on the work of folklorists, this chapter extends the conversation surrounding the folk poetry of childhood, examining the carnivalesque nature and knowledge-making potential of children's subversive and game-oriented rhymes, reminding us that children's poetry includes the work that is produced and disseminated by children, often outside of adult supervision.

Official school poetry and playground poetry exist on a spectrum. Somewhere between the two lies *domesticated* playground poetry, the subject of chapter 4. Domesticated playground poetry utilizes the carnivalesque tropes of playground poetry, but domesticates those tropes, sanitizing the poetry so as to make it appropriate for publication and purchase. The domesticated variety of playground poetry is either produced or approved by adults. Adult notions of decorum and propriety mediate domesticated playground poetry. Theodore Roethke and John Ciardi are some of the first poets in the United States to really explore this type of verse, though Jack Prelutsky and Shel Silverstein were to turn it into a market success.

Existing outside the spectrum of official school and playground poetry is visual poetry. Nowhere has concrete and visual poetry found a more comfortable and profitable home than in children's poetry. Chapter 5 places the concrete boom in children's publishing into the context of avant-garde visual poetry for adults in North America and the world. The chapter addresses why visual poems written for adults so often find their way into anthologies for children. Furthermore, it suggests the promise and the limitations of the genre through close readings of several visual texts.

Richard Flynn writes in "Can Children's Poetry Matter?" that poetry for U.S. children is "like poetry for adults [. . . ,] a clouded battleground for competing camps of poets with specific political or careerist agendas" (40). Certainly this is true. However, while the world of contemporary U.S. poetry for adults has been mapped repeatedly (if unsatisfactorily), the world of such poetry for children has not. This book seeks to extend the parameters and articulate more fully the issues suggested by previous scholarship of both children's poetry and adult poetry, braiding together these two strands of inquiry. It is a refiguring of the "competing camps" Flynn mentions, an attempt to better understand children's poetry and the children who read it, write it, and perform it in school, at home, and on the playground.

1

Public Poetry and Politics
Robert Frost and the Emerging Canon of Mid-Century American Children's Poetry

A golden age of poetry and power
Of which this noonday's the beginning hour.

Robert Frost, "For John F. Kennedy His Inauguration"

In the same year Robert Frost published his now classic *You Come Too: Favorite Poems for Young Readers* (1959), Randall Jarrell—with characteristic flair—proclaimed, "The public has an unusual relationship to the poet: it doesn't even know that he is there" ("Poets" 305). Five years later, in the year before his death, Jarrell would amend this statement, looking to Frost as a potential bridge between poets and the public, between poetry and politics. Reflecting on Frost's summer visit to the Soviet Union in 1962—particularly on Khrushchev's famous trip to Frost's sickbed in Gagra, Georgia—Jarrell writes that Frost "had helped to join power and poetry in this new age of Kennedy—couldn't his word to Khrushchev help transform the cold war into an honorable rivalry between the two great powers of the world?" (*Kipling* 368). Earlier, in his 1961 National Book Award acceptance speech, Jarrell commented on his delight in Kennedy's affection for poetry, his admirable invitation of Frost "to help inaugurate the president of the United States" (*Letters* 449). He continued, perhaps a little too optimistically, "It is a pleasure to think that for the next four or eight years our art and our government won't be complete strangers" (449).

Frost's words directly preceded the young president's oath of office on Inauguration Day, in a spectacle that still carries metaphoric resonance. In the years between 1959 and 1964 Frost's work was to become—and remains even today—a staple in the poetic diet of U.S. schoolchildren. However, it is important to view his relationship and centrality to the canon of children's poetry in the larger context of Frost's elevated reputation by

1

American critics, poets, and—curiously—the government itself. The social and political climate of the late '50s and early to mid '60s was integral to constructing Frost as *the* American school poet, a construction that has curious ideological implications concerning what is deemed appropriate poetry for U.S. children, especially when compared to the treatment in education textbooks of American poets Carl Sandburg and Gwendolyn Brooks.

Frost's reputation, of course, was already great at the end of the '50s, but it was made incontrovertibly permanent in those last years of his life, years that Jeffery Meyers writes "were like the explosion of a star before it dies" (*Frost* 321). At eighty-six years old, Frost established himself as the definitive American poet by giving his blessing and poetic insight to the new, youthful President Kennedy.[1] Later, on February 26, 1961, before a large television audience, Kennedy would look back on that breezy, bright January afternoon with the following words:

> I asked Robert Frost to come and speak at the inauguration not merely because I was desirous of according a recognition to his trade, but also because I felt he had something important to say to those of us who are occupied with the business of Government, that he would remind us that we were dealing with life, the hopes and fears of millions of people, and also to tell us that our own deep convictions must be the ultimate guide of all our actions. (125)

The apparent marriage of poetry and power of which Jarrell writes and Frost's cultural apotheosis followed the Eisenhower years—what Robert Lowell calls "the tranquillized *Fifties*" in "Memories of West Street and Lepke"—a markedly antipoetic decade (*Selected Poems* 91).[2] If, in the words of Bob Perelman, Kennedy's inauguration was "the high-water mark of cultural prestige for poetry in America" (111), then certainly it is a consequential moment in *children's* poetry in America as well. It is no coincidence that the poet Kennedy chose to speak to and for the nation is the same one that teachers, educators, and anthologists select to speak to and shape children. Just as Frost was the Grand Old Man of academic verse—he authored the introduction to Donald Hall, Louis Simpson, and Robert Pack's seminal *New Poets of England and America* (1957)[3]—he also became a kind of ambassador of poetry to both the government and schools, coming to represent what I call official school poetry.

In 1958 Frost became the poetry consultant at the Library of Congress, filling the vacancy left by Jarrell.[4] Roy Basler notes that Frost's

> presence on the Washington scene from 1958 through 1962 lent considerable impetus to the movement culminating in the establishment of the Kennedy Center and the National Foundation of the Arts and Humanities, [and] helped

bring about the continuing series of Cabinet- and White House–sponsored literary and performing arts presentations in the State Department Auditorium, and the White House receptions, dinners, presentations of awards, and festivals honoring prominent figures in the arts and humanities. (76)

However, often depicted as a man of "savage competitiveness" (Wilbur 182) and, in the words of Edmund Wilson, "one of the most relentless self-promoters in the history of American Literature" (qtd. in Meyers, *Wilson* 453), Frost had competition for the title of America's poet in the person of Carl Sandburg, an activist, biographer, poet, and children's author, whom Meyers aptly calls Frost's "popular rival," one who "equaled Frost's popularity among readers and on the lecture circuit" (*Frost* 81, 130). As Alan Golding points out, from 1934 to 1941 Sandburg was one of only three poets to appear in five major anthologies "ranging in their allegiances and selection criteria from the primarily aesthetic (*The Oxford Anthology of American Literature*) to the primarily political (*The Democratic Spirit*)" (110–11).[5] Penelope Niven writes that Sandburg had been commonly "hailed as the poet of the future, the poet of America" (376). Writing in 1953 about Sandburg's seventy-fifth birthday celebration, columnist Fanny Butcher referred to Sandburg as "America's cultural sweetheart," which, Philip R. Yannella notes, "summarized the feelings expressed in the testimonials given at the party" (xi), whose five hundred and some odd guests included "major politicians, foreign dignitaries, and famous scholars" (x).

Widely anthologized, Frost ascended in popularity in the '40s and '50s and actively sought a central place in the canon of American poets. Sandburg remained Frost's leading competitor, the two ranking among the most highly anthologized contemporary American poets of the mid-century.[6] Craig S. Abbott's "Modern American Poetry: Anthologies, Classroom, and Canons" (1990), a survey of high school textbooks, demonstrates that it was Sandburg rather than Frost who was the most widely anthologized poet for high school children from 1917 to 1934, with Frost a close second (210). Abbott writes, "[A]s late as 1960, the 72 multigenre high school anthologies then available presented a canon of Frost, Sandburg, Edna St. Vincent Millay, [. . .] [T. S.] Eliot, and [Amy] Lowell—Frost with 136 appearances, Lowell with 20" (210). In the present world of adult anthologies, however, Frost is unchallenged: in 1990 his "Stopping by Woods on a Snowy Evening"—a poem that Donald Hall writes "has *become* a poem for children" (*Oxford* xxxvi)—was the most commonly anthologized poem in the English language.[7]

From the beginning of their relationship (Frost was four years Sandburg's senior), there was between the two a contest of egos. Frost attacked—though behind genial humor—Sandburg's free verse and what he thought was a general lack of musicality, and he often found excuses to gibe Sandburg's undignified stage persona (Parini 416). Sandburg is on one end of the poetic continuum of the 1950s and '60s, tracing his poetic lineage (and his populist leanings) to the expansive free verse of Walt Whitman. On the other end we have Frost, who, in the words of Richard Gray, "is probably the greatest traditionalist in twentieth-century American poetry" (131). Both politically and poetically, Sandburg aligns nicely with what was to be called the "raw" school of poetry, just as Frost's traditionalism situates him as the elder spokesman of the "cooked" school.[8] In reply to Frost's famous statement "I had soon write free verse as play tennis with the net down" (*Poetry and Prose* 415), Sandburg insisted, "[Y]ou can play a better game with the net down." Frost rejoined, "Sure you can [. . .] and without the racket and balls—but it ain't tennis" (qtd. in Meyers, *Frost* 81).

While this may seem merely an aesthetic quarrel, the issue at the heart of this debate is ultimately political. Frost's concerns are methodological—how one writes poetry, how one determines what is "tennis" and what is not "tennis." Sandburg, in the Whitman tradition, is not playing "tennis" according to Frost's rules, rules championed by the New Critics. Of course, Frost was never a favorite of the New Critics. Though Frost was well represented in Cleanth Brooks and Robert Penn Warren's *Understanding Poetry* (1938)—a veritable treatise on New Critical pedagogy—Alan Golding argues that Frost's ample representation in this and later editions was more the outcome of Frost's already considerable reputation than Brooks's and Warren's fondness of him (106). However, Warren's belief that the "tension between the rhythm of the poem and the rhythm of speech" (*New and Selected Essays* 24) does help to "explain the textbook's (and general New Critical) preference for a simultaneously metrical and colloquial poet like Frost over the free verse of Whitman and Williams" and, no doubt, Sandburg (Golding 107). Golding remarks that the New Critical method that was so appropriate to much of Frost's work "leads to the exclusion of [William Carlos] Williams, of Whitman and nearly the whole Whitman tradition in American poetry, and of most free verse, of the poetry of most women and all minorities" (113). Until relatively recently, Langston Hughes, Gwendolyn Brooks, and later June Jordan and Nikki Giovanni, were all marginalized in both the canons of adult poetry and the canons of children's poetry, largely because of the overtly political nature and historical situatedness of their poetry. Like Sandburg's, their poetry is immensely political in theme and form.[9]

Sandburg preceded Frost into the realm of children's poetry, publishing *Early Moon*, his first book of poetry for children, in 1930. *Early Moon* was reprinted in 1958, a year before Frost's *You Come Too* and two years before Sandburg's last collection of poetry for children, *Wind Song* (1960).

In the introduction to *Early Moon*, "A Short Talk on Poetry," Sandburg defends free verse, arguing that though its modern incarnation may have risen "out of the machine age, skyscrapers, high speed and jazz," it is nonetheless found in the "earliest styles of poetry known to the human family," styles that he implies are profoundly political, styles that privilege freedom and play and reject (or at least question) "established and formal rules" (24). Take, for instance, "Soup"—an overtly political poem both formally and thematically—which is the last poem in the "Portraits" section of *Early Moon*. In this poem the speaker watches a public figure eating from a bowl of soup:

> I say he was lifting a fat broth
> Into his mouth with a spoon.
> His name was in the newspapers that day
> Spelled out in tall black headlines
> And thousands of people were talking about him.
> > When I saw him,
> He sat bending his head over a plate
> Putting soup in his mouth with a spoon. (2–9)

The paratactic sentences reject hierarchy and subordination and question the worship of those who are in power, those who are featured daily in the media. Furthermore, the poem privileges a populist "I," one whose views carry the same weight as the "tall black headlines": "*I say* he was lifting a fat broth." Indeed, the only subordinated clause is "When I saw him." Though he may appear larger than life in those "tall black headlines," when the lyric speaker sees him—and when the child reader sees him through the lyric speaker's eyes—this "famous man" is no more valuable than anyone who bends "his head over a plate," who puts "soup in his mouth with a spoon." In fact, the child (and adult) reader sees that the "famous man" is neither bigger nor better than we are and is perhaps no more deserving of those "tall black headlines" than any of the oft-ignored working class.

Other poems in the collection honor the worker and the working class. In "Manual System" Sandburg writes about Mary, an operator, who "has a thingamajig clamped on her ears / And sits all day taking plugs out and sticking plugs in" (1–2). Without her, the vast network of communication and exchange would fail, the "voices and voices / calling for ears to pour words in" would be unheard (3–4). In "Street Window" Sandburg reminds the child reader that "The pawn-shop man knows hunger, / And how far hunger has eaten the heart / Of one who comes with an old keepsake" (1–3). With the simple, elegant paradox of "hunger" feasting on the heart of the poor, Sandburg shows his empathy and concern for the working class, for the downtrodden. His poems concern the workers of urban and rural America, just as they glorify the urban and rural American landscape, recognizing overtly the heterogeneity of America. In "Illinois Farmer" he commands, "Bury this old Illinois Farmer with respect" (1).

Yet, again, in the New Critical climate of the mid-century, critics did not acclaim Sandburg's poetry—devoid as it often was of density, ambiguity, and irony—though vast numbers of readers still bought his work for themselves and their children. In a special Sandburg issue of *Voices: A Quarterly of Poetry* (1946), Henry W. Wells compares Sandburg to Wallace Stevens, who enjoyed a similar special issue a year earlier. Wells notes that Sandburg is often criticized for lacking "density" and "virtuosity"—the ability to "[compress] a maximum of meaning into a single word or phrase"—a virtuosity with which Stevens is also well equipped (41). Wells continues, "Although there has been much less praise or criticism of any sort for Sandburg, he has been more widely read. The professors read—and elucidate—Stevens. [. . . But] Sandburg is the most widely read American poet among the college students themselves. And there are always more students than teachers" (42). In short, Wells concludes, though Sandburg's verse "is clearly made of coarser stuff" than Stevens's, his poetry "broadcasts on a wavelength with a wider radius" (42). Although Wells is kinder to Sandburg than most academic commentators of the time, he nevertheless articulates the common view. In "Fifty Years of American Poetry," a talk presented on the first evening of the three-day 1962 National Poetry Festival in Washington, D.C., Randall Jarrell similarly speaks kindly of Sandburg, but ultimately denies that his work is poetry:

> Carl Sandburg's poems, generally, are improvisations whose wording is approximate; they do not have the exactness, the guaranteeing sharpness and strangeness of a real style. Sandburg is a colorful, appealing, and very American writer, so that you long for his little vignettes or big folk-editorials, with their easy sentimentality and easy idealism, to be made into finished works of art; but he sings songs more stylishly than he writes them, says his poems better than they are written—it is marvelous to hear him say "The People, Yes," but it is not marvelous to read it as a poem. (*National* 115)

One might amend this last sentence to "but it is not marvelous to read them as a New Critic would." The New Criticism had by the 1960s become the modus operandi of English studies.[10] Of course, Thomas Travisano argues in *Midcentury Quartet* (1999) that Jarrell's criticism was informed by a theory much more dialectical than that of his New Critical mentors John Crowe Ransom, Cleanth Brooks, and Allen Tate. Though Jarrell found their insistence on the preeminent value of irony, paradox, and poised ambiguity limiting, concerning Sandburg he sounds quite like his New Critical mentors, several of whom were in attendance at the festival.[11]

The New Critics, who were primarily interested in the explication of lyric poetry, concerned themselves with the analysis of poems as "verbal icons" unfettered by historical and social concerns.[12] Sandburg's poetry, simple, straightforward, declarative, and, most important, performative, did not resonate with the New Critics' aesthetic sensibilities, particularly their insistence on poetry as verbal icon. When Jarrell grants that "it is marvelous to hear [Sandburg] say 'The People, Yes,'" but critiques it for not being "marvelous [. . .] as a poem," he admits that as a verbal icon it is not interesting, while as a performance it is. Much of Sandburg's poetry depends on performance, not on poised tension, on stasis. In this respect Sandburg writes in the spirit of the playground poetry discussed in chapter 3, a mode of poetry that is different from official school poetry. Of course, Jarrell evaluated Frost—whom he came to appreciate only late in life—more favorably in his talk. Frost, whom Kennedy biographer Richard Reeves calls "the unofficial poet laureate of the [Kennedy] administration," was the keynote speaker and read from his verse the second night of the poetry festival (350). Sandburg, who was invited, did not attend, presumably, as Mary Jarrell reports the rumors, because he "would never share honors with Frost" (*Letters* 458). Jarrell's sentiments are a useful barometer of Sandburg's reputation among American poets and critics of the day.

Frost's "apolitical" tendencies made him a more likely choice for participating in the Kennedy inauguration in 1961, despite the fact that the immensely popular Sandburg supported Kennedy's campaign for president and was already famous for reading at Adlai Stevenson's 1949 inauguration as Illinois's governor.[13] Sandburg was a potentially volatile choice, one who characterized himself in the 1920s as "a socialist but not a member of the party." He continues, in characteristic paratactic style, "I am an I. W. W. but I don't carry a red card. I am an anarchist but not a member of the organization. [. . .] I belong to everything and nothing. [. . .] I am with all rebels everywhere all the time as against all people who are satisfied" (qtd. in Niven 346)—people, no doubt, like the "famous man" supping on his "fat broth" in the poem "Soup"; people, perhaps, like the extravagant Kennedys. Sandburg "was a personality on early television," appearing on the "Ed Sullivan, Milton Berle, Dave Garroway, Ernie Kovacs, and Edward R. Murrow shows" (Yannella ix). Yet despite his popularity—or perhaps because of it—Sandburg found himself scrutinized by the FBI as a potential communist sympathizer and found that the "socialist idealism he had espoused at the turn of the century" (Niven 337) was not welcomed even in post-McCarthy America. Sandburg celebrated the worker at a time when the establishment feared a workers' party. For example, in "People Who Must" (which appeared in *Early Moon*), Sandburg characterizes for his child readers a steeplejack who, high above the busy city streets, "painted on the roof of a skyscraper," proudly reflecting, "I painted a long while and called it a day's work" (1–2). Yet the popular Sandburg was invited to Kennedy's inauguration nonetheless, probably because of the president's fondness of his work.[14] However, Sandburg declined to attend.

Of course, personal preference played a large role in Kennedy's selection of Frost for the inaugural reading. In his 1961 National Book Award acceptance speech, Jarrell perceptively noted that Kennedy invited Frost to read "not as a friend, not as a politician, but as a reader: any of us who heard the president talk about Frost's poetry, on television [. . .] will remember that he spoke as only a real reader of Frost could speak, and read the lines as Frost himself would have read them" (*Letters* 449). On the television program of which Jarrell speaks, "Robert Frost: American Poet," Kennedy says:

> Perhaps the rarest courage of all—for the skill to pursue it is given to a very few men—is the courage to wage a silent battle to illuminate the nature of man and the world in which he lives. [. . .] Robert Frost is often characterized as an American poet—or a New England poet. And he is of course, all of these things, for the temper of his region and of his Nation has provided a good deal of meter and the tone in which he has dealt. But he is not a poet bounded by geography. He will live as a poet of the life of man, of the darkness and despair, as well as of the hope—which is, in his case, limited by a certain skepticism—and also for his wit and understanding of man's limitations[,] which lie behind all of man's profoundest statements. (125)[15]

The language in this excerpt is clear: Frost, one of those "few men" who are able, speaks to "*man's* limitations," utters and understands "*man's* profoundest statements," and sheds light on "*the* nature of man." He is not "bounded by geography": he speaks for us all—*us,* of course, referring to white, male Americans. There is, Kennedy suggests, but one "nature of man," and that, it appears, is the nature of the New England folk who people Frost's work. Kennedy politicizes Frost by constructing him as a universal poet, one who speaks for humanity, for all Americans.[16] These qualities are those that make Frost, in the eyes of anthologists and teachers, such an appropriate poet for children. Yet Kennedy also notes many of the same qualities Jarrell outlines in "The Other Frost" (1947), the "darkness and despair" that is evident throughout Frost's oeuvre, the "hope [. . .] limited by a certain skepticism" that tempers the darkness, as well as his superb "wit and understanding."

However, even putting Kennedy's insights about Frost aside, there was suspicion among the Left that his preoccupation with the arts—and Frost in particular—was merely, as Robert Lowell blatantly put it, "window dressing."[17] The Frost that Kennedy summoned to the inauguration was the rustic New England Frost, not the dark, skeptical Frost so evident in his poetry. In his speech Kennedy associates New England with American high culture, with a poet "not [. . .] bounded by geography," while simultaneously using this association to link himself with that culture, adding to the mystique of what would come to be termed Camelot. In *J.F.K.: The Man and the Myth* (1963), Victor Lasky points to Fulton Lewis, Jr., who on January 25, 1961, wrote in the *Exclusive*, "The invitation to Robert Frost for a special Inaugural poem somehow smacked of a Poet Laureate in the British royal tradition" (qtd. in Lasky 12). Although Jarrell was undoubtedly correct in his belief that Kennedy was "a real reader of Frost," Lasky notes, "There was something strangely symbolic about the entire episode," something that smacked of political maneuvering (20). Lasky continues, "Kennedy had asked Frost to change the last line of 'The Gift Outright' [the poem Frost recited from memory that day] in order to remind listeners of the New Frontier" (20). Concerning the proposed change, the *Economist*'s Washington correspondent wrote, "It is not a change which a man with an instinct for poetry, as distinct from propaganda, would have asked for." He continues, suggesting, "The episode seems to illustrate the chilliness and calculation which some people detect in Kennedy" (qtd. in Lasky 20).[18] It also illustrates John McClure's assessment of Kennedy's self-conception, a two-part narrative in which "Kennedy [. . .] appears to remind America of her high destiny," and then leads the "reawakened nation [. . .] adventuring across the new frontiers of the times" (43).

Yet the United States public still saw Frost primarily as an apolitical poet who spoke timeless truths in clear, finely wrought lines. This conservative view troubled many of Frost's contemporaries in the world of poetry and the academy. Biographer Allan Seager writes that Theodore Roethke had by 1961 "long since lost his respect for Frost as a poet, saying that his New England was a mere literary convention" (278).[19] Indeed, in a move designed to counteract Frost's innocuous, bucolic image, Lionel Trilling rearticulated Jarrell's 1947 thesis (without mentioning Jarrell by name) that beneath Frost's seemingly tranquil poetry there is a dark undercurrent concerned with "the representation of the terrible actualities of life in a new way" (qtd. in Meyers, *Frost* 318). However, this "terrible Frost" is sublimated in works aimed at teachers of children, works in which we see Frost cast as a wise Everyman who speaks for us all, the idealized Frost of the Kennedy inauguration. The third edition of May Hill Arbuthnot's popular education textbook *Children and Books* (1964), released the year after Frost's death, exemplifies this tendency. Arbuthnot, a well-known teacher, lecturer, and author, was at the peak of her career during this time (she died in 1969) and was quite influential in educational circles. According to her introductory note to the third edition, *Children and Books* "was planned as a text-book for children's literature courses in English and education departments and in library training schools of colleges and universities" (n.p.). She notes, however, that her book has proved "helpful" to a wider audience, one including "[p]arents, camp directors, and Sunday-school teachers" (n.p.).

Children and Books is representative of the view educators took of Frost after the explosive fame the 1960s afforded him. Arbuthnot writes that Frost speaks "for America in the rhythms and idiom of American speech" (186). This is an odd claim, especially as Frost is noted for his skill at rendering in metered lines the pronounced, regional speech patterns of rustic New England. Nevertheless, Arbuthnot tells her readers, "To have heard [Frost] read his own poems was to hear America talking—not urban or academic America, but the America of farmers, villagers, people close to the earth" (187). One suspects that Arbuthnot means "real" Americans, not the Americans to which a poet like Sandburg might speak, and certainly not those peopling Gwendolyn Brooks's audience.

In the 1964 edition of *Children and Books,* Frost provides the gravitational center for the sections on poetry. Arbuthnot's choice of Frost as this central icon serves a political agenda similar to Kennedy's. She begins her discussion of Frost by writing, "Robert Frost is *the* American poet our children should grow up to, and that means with" (186, emphasis mine) and spends three pages introducing Frost to her readers. Her treatment of Frost suggests that he has always been part of the children's poetry canon, always been an institution, a necessary part of all American children's reading. Curiously, however, in the previous edition of *Children and Books* (1957), Arbuthnot mentions Frost only once, though by that time he had won the Pulitzer prize four times. Of course, the 1957 edition of *Children and Books* predates Frost's appointment as the Library of Congress's poetry consultant (1958), *You Come Too* (1959), and the Kennedy inaugural reading, three factors that doubtlessly led to Frost's replacement of Sandburg as "school poet." But Louis Untermeyer's immensely popular illustrated Frost primer, *Come In and Other Poems* (1943), had been in circulation for more than ten years, as had nearly all the poems that would be included in *You Come Too.* When Frost is mentioned in the 1957 edition, Arbuthnot calls his words "cryptic" (195). She quotes Frost concerning the nature of poetry: "Robert Frost, in a series of cryptic comments on poetry, said: 'The eye reader is a barbarian. So also is the writer for the eye reader, who needn't care how badly he writes since he doesn't care how badly he is read'" (195). With that she leaves Frost and continues discussing how to engender in children a love of poetry. She discusses none of his poems and does not linger to unpack his "cryptic" claims or relate them to Frost's pet theory of the "sound of sense." Yet, as we have seen, after Frost's adoption as the nation's poet in 1961, Arbuthnot uses Frost extensively, if, regrettably, no more critically.

In the 1964 edition Arbuthnot dwells on poems like "Stopping by Woods on a Snowy Evening" and especially "The Gift Outright," which, she says, "is a perfect example of Frost's own pronouncement that 'Each poem clarifies something'" (205). "The Gift Outright," one of Frost's most politically charged poems, first appeared in *The Witness Tree* (1942), though it was reprinted in Frost's last collection, *In the Clearing* (1962).[20] It was famous at the time for being the poem Frost recited from memory at Kennedy's inauguration, and in *Children and Books* Arbuthnot uses the poem as an occasion to meditate on what it means to be an American, encouraging us to see in it the "easy sentimentality and easy idealism" that Jarrell complains of in Sandburg's writings. The poem begins:

> The land was ours before we were the land's.
> She was our land more than a hundred years
> Before we were her people. She was ours
> In Massachusetts, in Virginia,
> But we were still England's, still colonials,
> Possessing what we still were unpossessed by[.] (1–6)

As Bob Perelman notes, the opening conceit equates American soil with femininity, "making us a corporate male that needs to make her ours; and the passage of historical time gives way to the drama of sexualized geopolitical possession with only a before and an after" (112). Moreover, any peoples who may have occupied the land before "we" arrived are evident only in their absence, and the whole of American history is rendered as the expansionist impulse of Anglo-Americans:

> Such as we were we gave ourselves outright
> (The deed of gift was many deeds of war)
> To the land vaguely realizing westward[.] (12–14)

Perelman writes, "The mention of war only in parentheses and the cloudy uplift of language keep particulars at bay" (112). Arbuthnot's commentary on the poem minimizes Frost's parenthetical treatment of our nation's wars, a treatment that neatly elides the horror of war. Perhaps with an eye toward potential history lessons, Arbuthnot writes, "The children can readily fill in the wars involved in '(The deed of gift was many deeds of war)'" (204).

However, she suggests that teachers should not linger on that line, for "it is more important to challenge the children with those enigmatic last lines—'Such as she was, such as she would become'" (204).[21] One might ask why those last lines are more important, especially as the poem's title includes the word *gift,* suggesting with dark irony that at least one of the gifts outright might be war. Indeed, during his reading at the National Poetry Festival, Frost himself, after reading this very poem, reiterated that line, saying, "And you know, the part that some people wouldn't notice so much: 'The deed of gift was many deeds of war . . .' we threw our lives right into it" (254). In short, Arbuthnot's treatment of Frost's poem reinforces an uncomplicated notion of Manifest Destiny. At a time when U.S. interests were "vaguely realizing westward" to Vietnam and upward to the moon, when U.S. education budgets were swelling, it makes sense that Arbuthnot would foreground an uncomplicated view of this patriotic poem while downplaying poets like Brooks and Sandburg, who were more overtly critical of the status quo. After all, the cold war had been heating up in recent years: the Berlin Wall and the Cuban missile crises weren't too long past, and Robert Lowell wasn't the only American made uncomfortable by the "chafe and jar / of nuclear war" (as he wrote in his poem "Fall 1961.") Frost's work was relatively untouched by the specifics of cold war anxiety, even if Frost was not, and thus his poems were a welcome addition to the classroom.

Unlike Frost, Brooks and Sandburg, both Illinois laureates (Brooks succeeded Sandburg as laureate in 1968), have been generally seen as regional poets, poets of the Midwest. They are featured in Arbuthnot's 1964 textbook—Brooks in the section "New Singers of Small Songs" (Brooks was, incidentally, forty-six years old at the time) and Sandburg in "Poets of the Child's World." The anthology dedicates two paragraphs to Brooks, who does not appear in the 1957 edition, and her work is characterized by two poems, "Cynthia in the Snow" and "Vern." Arbuthnot emphasizes Brooks's ethnicity, while insisting that despite it, children of "any race" can enjoy her poetry. She writes, "A Negro poet, Gwendolyn Brooks, has twice been recipient of a Guggenheim Fellowship. She has also received the Pulitzer Prize for [. . .] *Annie Allen*. [. . .] Her book of poems for and about children, *Bronzeville Boys and Girls* [1956], will have a universal appeal because the poems speak for any child of any race" (158). However, "Cynthia in the Snow" isn't as "universal" as Arbuthnot suggests. Rather, it is a highly situated poem, one that foregrounds the marginalized subjectivity of the speaker. "Cynthia in the Snow" sketches a particular child in a particular historical moment. Whether Arbuthnot fails to recognize the social dimensions of the poem or whether she simply wants to avoid the issue of race in her textbook is unclear. What is clear is that "Cynthia in the Snow" is profoundly political—as is, perhaps to a lesser degree, "Vern."

Unlike Arbuthnot, Doris M. King, in her 1957 review of *Bronzeville Boys and Girls* for the black quarterly *Phylon,* noticed the "social implications" of the poems, yet she, oddly enough, considered these implications *flaws* (94). In his essay "The Kindergarten of New Consciousness," Richard Flynn writes that King "chided the poet" for introducing, in her words, "a note of social comment" into her children's poems, a site, evidently, where such comments do not belong (492). King's conception of childhood—and by extension children's poetry—is unabashedly romantic. She suggests that Brooks's poems are at their best when they capture "the universal wonder of childhood," when they treat—"unfettered by social implications"—"those untranslatable people who 'come trailing clouds of glory'" (93, 94). Finally, she makes the curious claim that the most accomplished poems in *Bronzeville Boys and Girls* "are not about Bronzeville boys and girls, but simply boys and girls" (94). Flynn points to this review as an example of "the difficulty Brooks faced in disrupting the idealizing and sentimental view of childhood endorsed by mainstream culture in the '50s" (492). Even in the black press, we see the presence of dominant, mid-century American attitudes toward children's innocence. These attitudes, Flynn maintains, are "condescending and universalizing" (492), attitudes that treat politics and so called adult issues (including sex, death, and money) as strictly off-limits for children.

Arbuthnot seems to see "Cynthia in the Snow" and "Vern" as depoliticized poems about "untranslatable people" trailing Wordsworthian "clouds of glory." She claims that they are "in contrasting mood" (158), one positive ("Cynthia in the Snow"), one negative ("Vern"). Read politically, however, the poems seem of a piece; both deal with the child's fear of being alone, being an outsider, being without the security and creature comforts of the dominant world of 1950s white America. A close reading suggests that "Cynthia in the Snow" is less a lovely portrait of a child wondering at snow than it is a poignant metaphor for being black in a white culture, about finding oneself unsatisfactory because of one's color. The white snow "SUSHES" in all caps; it "hushes," indicating a silencing (1–2). The speaker continues:

> [It] laughs away from me.
> It laughs a lovely whiteness,
> And whitely whirs away,
> To be
> Some otherwhere,
> Still white as milk or shirts.
> So beautiful it hurts. (5–11)

13

The child speaker desires the snow, "white as milk or shirts," associated with nourishment, with cleanliness. It "flitter-twitters" away "whitely." It is "lovely" and "beautiful." The snow and the whiteness it represents call attention to Cynthia's own dark skin, her feelings of inadequacy, feelings that are cold and hurtful. Certainly this is not a poem that "speak[s] for a child of any race" (158), but instead is a poem speaking for the children of Bronzeville, the disadvantaged children of Southside Chicago, not those of New England, not those of white America generally. Of course, Brooks had not yet been radicalized by her attendance at the 1967 Fisk University Writers' Conference in Nashville. But it is a curious coincidence that while discussing whiteness and blackness in her autobiography, *Report from Part One* (1972), Brooks quotes her "little green *Webster's New World*['s]" definition of "white": "having the color of pure snow or milk" (83). She writes, "Until 1967 my own blackness did not confront me with a shrill spelling of itself" (83), and in this poem we see the whiteness of the snow dampening somewhat that shrill spelling, even as it is "SUSHING"—with its curious suggestion of "slush" and "shush"—Cynthia. However, though the snow "SUSHES" and "hushes," the child is *not* silenced. Cynthia still speaks. The poem is in first person: Cynthia articulates her discomfort, her hurt, through imaginative, poetic play. Indeed, in 1950, as her contribution to *Phylon's* symposium "The Negro Writer," Brooks wrote that black Americans like Cynthia, or indeed any of the children peopling *Bronzeville Boys and Girls,* "cannot escape having important things to say. [Their] mere bod[ies], for that matter, [are] an eloquence. [Their] quiet walk down the street is a speech to the people" (312).

In this respect, our fictional Cynthia is like Brooks herself, who read at the 1962 National Poetry Festival along with Frost, Jarrell, and many others, becoming, as William McGuire notes, "the first black poet to read publicly at the Library of Congress since Paul Laurence Dunbar in the 1880s" (243).[22] If, as Brooks maintains, the "Negro's" very walk "Is a rebuke, is a plea, is a school," then she was in some respects schooling her fellow poets, for she read poems that exemplified her belief that the black poet should "polish his technique" in order to better "[present] his truths and his beauties, that these may be more insinuating, and, therefore, more overwhelming" ("Poets" 312). Brooks's selections for the reading testify to her interest in childhood. Of all the poets at the festival, Brooks was the only one to read a children's poem. She read "Nora," from *Bronzeville Boys and Girls,* which she dedicated to her "little girl" (*National* 163). Even her choices from her adult work concerned children: the selections she read from her Pulitzer prize–winning *Annie Allen* (1949) were a trio of sonnets from "The Children of the Poor." Brooks does not shy away from depicting poor and disadvantaged children in either her adult or her children's poetry. In *Bronzeville*

Boys and Girls "Cynthia in the Snow" immediately precedes "John, Who Is Poor."

"Vern," the other poem Arbuthnot chose to represent Brooks, deals with a child feeling estranged from his world. In "Vern" Brooks writes that when one is unhappy, when even the elements seem to conspire against you, "A pup's a good companion— / If a pup you've got" (3, 4). The poem continues, describing how

> A pup will let you look at him,
> And even let you hold
> His little wiggly warmness—
>
> And let you snuggle down beside.
> Nor mock the tears you have to hide. (8–12)

However, the fourth line lingers: "If a pup you've got," reminding the reader that there are some people who are without even a puppy's small comfort, that there are some like John, of whom you should never "ask when his hunger will end, / Nor yet when it began" (7, 8).

Arbuthnot's treatment of Sandburg is equally interesting and, like her treatment of Frost, shifts considerably from the 1957 to the 1964 edition. As in Brooks's case, Arbuthnot's treatment of Sandburg shows how the political climate in the early '60s influenced how poets came to be represented. This lengthy quotation from the 1957 edition of *Children and Books* conveys Arbuthnot's approval of Sandburg and his populist poetry:

> The publication of his *Chicago Poems* in 1915 created a sensation and brought down upon [Sandburg's] head a fair balance of hostility and enthusiasm. Critics seemed to feel either that poetry was going rapidly downhill or that here was another Walt Whitman, a prophet of a new day. The poems were as lusty and gusty as the city they celebrated. His satire was robust, and he used strong, hard words.
>
> [. . . Sandburg's] vernacular seems natural today, but at the time his poems appeared it shocked many people and he was accused of unnecessary roughness. That criticism is hardly just, for Sandburg has a great range of both subject matter and style. In describing the cities of belching smokestacks, steel furnaces, and stockyards, he does use harsh words and lines and cadences that fall like hammer blows. But when he speaks of vast prairies or of "sleepy Henry Hackerman hoeing" or of milk on a baby's chin, his words are appropriately serene, his tempos slow-moving and easy. In short, he adapts his style to his theme. (154)

This defense continues for two more paragraphs, in which Arbuthnot argues for the sophistication of Sandburg's poems, for their "vigor and realism" (154). She does make the problematic claim that "many of Sandburg's poems are too mature and too concerned with sociological problems to be suitable for children," but she nevertheless insists that "many are worth trying with eleven- and twelve-year-olds and older" (154). Elsewhere in the book, Sandburg, who is referenced in six places, fills the role Frost attains in the next edition. While discussing *The American Songbag,* she writes, "[Sandburg's] writing has been concerned from first to last with the people, places, and spirit of the United States" (93). Later she pairs Sandburg with Mary Austin, writing that "both are difficult writers for children, with only a few poems which they accept wholeheartedly, but the best work of these two poets is too good to be overlooked" (158).

However, in the 1964 edition Arbuthnot cools somewhat toward Sandburg. No musings on Sandburg's concern for "the people, places, and spirit of the United States" appear in this edition's much briefer treatment of *The American Songbag.* In the discussion of Sandburg's poetry, we see some telling editorial changes. From the 1957 edition: "Critics seemed to feel either that poetry was going rapidly downhill or that here was another Walt Whitman, a prophet of a new day. The poems were as lusty and gusty as the city they celebrated. His satire was robust, and he used strong, hard words" (154). From the 1964 edition: "Critics seemed to feel either that poetry was going rapidly downhill or that here was another Walt Whitman, a prophet of a new day. So with readers today, either they like Sandburg's gusty, lusty verse or they find it contrived, self-conscious, and continually disappointing" (145). Whereas in the 1957 edition Arbuthnot claims the criticism leveled against Sandburg is "hardly just," and continues for two paragraphs in Sandburg's defense, in the 1964 edition she limits her words to "His two books for children will be so evaluated, plus or minus. However, the books are worth trying with eleven- and twelve-year-olds" (145). She then provides a short list of poems that children may or may not like. No doubt Sandburg's socialist leanings played a part in Arbuthnot's cooling, just as Frost's apparent apolitical nature and fame made him an easy replacement. Basler himself notes how closely the two poets were linked in the minds of the nation, explaining, somewhat ironically, how easy their situations could have been switched: "Among my thoughts [after Frost's inaugural reading] was the whimsical reflection, which I voiced as we trudged away to watch the parade: 'I guess it was a good thing Adlai was defeated in 1952, or Carl might have been the Prairie Vergil of the "next Augustan age"'" (75).

Thus we see how Brooks's poetry was depoliticized, Sandburg's poetry fell from esteem, and Frost's poetry replaced Sandburg's as a necessary part of all American children's poetic diet. And though the political climate that produced Frost's new role in the education of children may have changed since the 1960s, the role Frost's work took on during that time remains unchanged. Of course, Frost had been interested in education from the beginnings of his career, but surely it is more than coincidence that he became emblematic of official school poetry during the same period Kennedy adopted him as unofficial laureate. However, his longevity as such a central figure in school poetry may be attributed to factors other than politics. Throughout his career, Frost consistently advocated the use of poetry in schools, and in his famous "Education by Poetry" (1931) he lamented how educators are prone to treat poetry "as if it were something else than poetry, as if it were syntax, language, science" (34). A champion of the complexity of poetry, of the irreducibility of poetry, Frost believed that "Poetry begins in trivial metaphors, pretty metaphors, 'grace' metaphors, and goes on to the profoundest thinking that we have" (36). Surely his poetry demonstrates a degree of this profundity, and the critics are right to recognize the formal and thematic complexity in it. Yet it is an irony that one of the apparent reasons his work has found such a home in primary and secondary education is its teachability. In his posthumously published "Levels and Opposites: Structure in Poetry," Jarrell writes, "metre, stanza form, rhyme, alliteration, quantity, and so on" are the least important qualities of poetry, qualities that "criticism has paid [. . .] an altogether disproportionate amount of attention [to]—partly, I suppose, because they are things any child can point at, draw diagrams of, and count" (697). Of course, they are also matters on which teachers can lecture and for which they can test and evaluate. As well as being teachable, Frost's poems largely sidestep the "sociological problems" that Arbuthnot notices in Sandburg's poetry, as they similarly avoid the vexing political and racial issues raised by Brooks. Furthermore, the subtlety of Frost's thinking is easy to miss, and his ambiguity is often difficult to excavate.

In the ninth edition of *Children and Books* (1997), edited by Zena Sutherland (who joined Arbuthnot with the fourth edition), Frost is the first poet mentioned in the "Poetry" chapter. Sutherland gives to future teachers their first definition of poetry from Frost, who writes, "[A] poem is a momentary stay against confusion. Each poem clarifies something. [. . .] A poem is an arrest of disorder" (271). Indeed, this is the same quotation Arbuthnot uses to praise "The Gift Outright" (which is not mentioned in the ninth edition). Immediately after Sutherland's discussion of Frost comes Sandburg, and his treatment is briefer than in the third edition. Oddly, as an example of his "robust simplicity" Sutherland chooses "Bubbles," a piece featuring a speaking bubble—certainly not the most representative of Sandburg's poems. Brooks's treatment is much the same as well. Sutherland acknowledges that Brooks's poems show a "concern for racial and personal identity," but removes "Vern" and holds to Arbuthnot's problematic claim that the poems in *"Bronzeville Boys and Girls* [. . .] speak for any child of any race" (300). Certainly they may speak *to* any child of any race, but Brooks's primary project seems to involve giving voice to a relatively silenced group, the children of Bronzeville.

Frost's continued preeminence in the canon of children's poets is also evident in contemporary critical essays and books about children's poetry. The third edition of *Only Connect,* a collection of forty-two critical essays concerning children's literature, contains only two essays about poetry. The first, by Myra Cohn Livingston, is titled "The Poem on Page 81" and uses Frost's "The Pasture" as a central organizing force and as an example of rich, complicated children's poetry. The second, by X. J. Kennedy, concerns American nonsense poetry. *Only Connect* suggests what I will argue are the two dominant modes of children's poetry: official school poetry, or the poetry of the classroom (exemplified by Frost), and a rather defanged poetry of the playground, exemplified by poets such as Ciardi, Silverstein, and Prelutsky.[23]

Gregory Denman's *When You've Made It Your Own: Teaching Poetry to Young People* (1988), a short education textbook on poetry, epitomizes works that construct and entrench the hierarchy discussed earlier. Denman's text implies this hierarchy by constructing Frost as an emblem of official school poetry and castigating teachers who would teach Silverstein. Denman opines that Silverstein's poems "hardly have to be taught: Put them in the hands of children and they teach themselves" (xvii). He assumes that if his students do not know Frost, they do not know any poetry. Certainly some students might not know Frost and the official school poetry he represents, but they do have access to an intricate poetry of their own—the poetry of the playground, a type of poetry that is wholly ignored by Denman. However, Denman does not ignore Frost, finding occasion to reference him some fifteen times in his text, going as far as to joke, "I always explained straight-faced to my big, sophisticated fifth graders that they would be in a fair amount of trouble if they could not abide by the school rules, but if anyone, at any time, under any circumstances, said anything bad about Robert Frost . . . well, we're talking about immediate suspension from school. Needless to say, my kids loved old Bob Frost" (64). Though Denman is joking (quite condescendingly), Frost clearly represents the poetic establishment. Frost has become an icon, venerable, unquestionable. Frost's centrality to the children's poetry canon illustrates tellingly how overt politics and children's poetry do not mix in official school poetry. Or, more precisely, how the politics of school poetry pretends to be invisible—either erased like Brooks's or pushed aside like Sandburg's.

2

"Levels and Opposites" in Randall Jarrell's *The Bat-Poet*

Two poetries are now competing, a cooked and a raw. The cooked, marvelously expert, often seems laboriously concocted to be tasted and digested by a graduate seminar. The raw, huge, blood-dripping gobbets of unseasoned experiences dished up for midnight listeners. . . . I exaggerate, of course.

Robert Lowell, 1960 National Book Award acceptance speech

Even as Robert Frost's reputation as America's poet—and indeed America's school poet—solidified in the late '50s and early '60s, a profound schism appeared in the world of adult poetry in America. During this time Randall Jarrell was one of the preeminent critics of American poetry and was certainly a well-established poet. He attended closely to the contemporary scene and in no small part helped write the canon of American poetry.[1] While several primarily adult poets were beginning to write for children at this time—notably John Ciardi, whose first book for children, *The Reason for the Pelican,* was published in 1959—Jarrell's forays into children's poetry are considerably different from most.[2] Unlike Ciardi, Theodore Roethke, and, later, X. J. Kennedy, who produced slim poetry books that in design at least were reminiscent of their adult work, Jarrell couched his poetry in the context of fairy tale–like prose narratives. He used these tales—specifically *The Bat-Poet* (1964)—to work through his theoretical notions of poetry, exploring the postmodern tendencies of contradiction and opposition that are also apparent in his adult work. In *The Bat-Poet* Jarrell's poetical investigations specifically center on navigating the schism that was evident in the so-called anthology wars, the opening skirmish of which was the publication of Donald Hall, Robert Pack, and Louis Simpson's anthology *The New Poets of England and America* (1957).

The poets included in this anthology, as Harvey Shapiro notes in a 1960 review, represent a sampling of those who were "working in the kitchens of the 'cooked' school" (6). This poetry anthology was answered three years later with the publication of Donald Allen's *The New American Poetry* (1960), representing the "raw" school—a group of poets who, in the words of Kenneth Koch, proclaimed, "GOODBYE, castrati of poetry! farewell stale pale skunky pentameters (the only honest English meter, gloop gloop!)" (Allen 236). On March 23, 1960, during his National Book Award acceptance speech, Jarrell's good friend Robert Lowell, who appears in Hall's anthology, delineated these two competing types of poetry: "a poetry of pedantry and a poetry of scandal" (qtd. in Mariani 282). Borrowing his terminology from Claude Levi-Strauss's *The Raw and the Cooked,* Lowell quipped that the cooked poetry was "expert and remote," resembling a metaphoric "mechanical or catnip mouse for graduate seminars." The raw poetry, on the other hand, "jerry-built and forensically deadly," was "often like an unscored libretto by some bearded but vegetarian Castro" (qtd. in Mariani 282).[3] Bitterly sarcastic about the cooked school, Koch characterizes the "young poets" of this camp in his poem "Fresh Air," calling them "worms" who "trembl[e] in their universities, [. . .] bathing the library steps with their spit [. . .] / / wish[ing] to perfect their form" (Allen 230). This poetic war heralded a spectacular shift in North American poetry. It would be an oversimplification to say that these anthologies and the two major camps they represented polarized North American poets. Nevertheless, many poets and schools of poets began to be assigned allegiances based on the poetics implied in the Hall, Pack, and Simpson anthology and those that were explicitly—if briefly—stated in the final section of the Allen anthology. Even today, so-called Language and post-Language poets trace their lineage to the New American school, just as the New Formalists look to the Hall, Pack, and Simpson anthology for their forebears.[4]

Born May 6, 1914, in Nashville, Tennessee, Jarrell was three years too old to appear in Hall's anthology, for the twenty-eight-year-old Hall included only writers "who [were] under forty" (9). It is more likely that Jarrell would have appeared in Hall's anthology than in Allen's, because, despite his affinity for the work of William Carlos Williams, Jarrell had little love for the work of the Beats, Projectivists, Black Mountain, and New York school poets who were featured in *New American Poetry.* However, as I will argue, Jarrell's poetic is more open to the play between the raw and the cooked than one might expect, and certainly he did not see fit to take sides in the raw and cooked debate. In 1958, for example, he wrote Karl Shapiro, "I wish all the San Francisco poets would eat all the University poets and burst, so that Nature, abhorring a vacuum, would send one plain poet or cat or rat to take their place" (*Letters* 436).

Yet as early as 1942 Jarrell was producing a body of work that resisted the binary logic that would come to be implied by the so-called anthology wars. This resistance can be seen in Jarrell's well-known essay "The End of the Line" (1942), in which he dismantles the then popular thesis that "modernist poetry is a revolutionary departure from the romantic poetry of the preceding century" (76). The essay collapses the romantic/modernist binary, blatantly stating that "It is the end of the line" for modernist poetry, that modernism, rather than being a departure from romanticism, has in fact carried romantic "tendencies to their limits" (81, 82). Furthermore, the essay implies that it was time for a new, postmodern poetic. Indeed, Jarrell explicitly called for this poetic two years earlier in "A Note on Poetry" (1940), where he writes, "During the course of the article, the reader may have thought curiously, 'Does he really suppose he writes the sort of poetry that replaces modernism?' Let me answer, like the man in the story, 'I must decline the soft impeachment.' But I am sorry I need to" (51). This remark prompted John Crowe Ransom to claim that if Jarrell, in 1940, was not already "post-modernist," then he "probably [. . .] will be" (15), giving us, as Thomas Travisano reminds, the "earliest documented use of the much debated term [. . .] in a literary context" ("Randall Jarrell" 695). Travisano notes that until recently most critics assumed Jarrell's poetic—as suggested by his criticism and embodied in his poetry—was "solely the product of intuition" and ultimately "lacked a theoretical center" (695). However, in Jarrell's recently rediscovered and posthumously published talk "Levels and Opposites: Structure in Poetry" (1942), Jarrell outlines a dialectical theory of poetry, one that makes the startlingly postmodern claim that "there are no things in a poem, only processes," that a poem is a dynamic function that hinges upon opposition, that it is as "static as an explosion" (697).[5]

Jarrell's views on poetry were radical for his time, as they reject the myopic views of the New Critics, whom he saw as a species of what might be called neo-neoclassicism.[6] In "Levels and Opposites" Jarrell critiques the New Critics' desire for unity in poetry, arguing that "some piece of Sunday-school didacticism and abstraction, limp, static, entirely lifeless, may nevertheless be beautifully unified" (699). He continues with characteristic wit: "The critic with neoclassic leanings will look at its neat correct logical structure, that fits its neat correct metrical and stanzaic structure so exactly—he will stare at these perfections, as proper as those of a Spenser sonnet—and he will wonder why, in spite of all its morality and logic and unity, it cannot affect even him" (699). His radical views undoubtedly led to the cold reception his Princeton talk received, the reception Travisano speculates may have led him to jot "Crit. is impossible" atop the manuscript he used for his presentation ("Randall Jarrell" 692–93). By the 1940s the New Criticism had begun its ascendancy, and already Jarrell was finding it too limiting a method. As we saw in chapter 1, the New Critics concerned themselves primarily with the explication of poems as unified "verbal icons." Even before

New Criticism had naturalized itself as *the* method of interpretation, Jarrell was criticizing its "tremendous emphasis on the irony and ambiguity of poetry" (704). Jarrell found the New Critical obsession with irony, paradox, and ambiguity somewhat shortsighted.

In "Levels and Opposites" Jarrell writes:

> Critics like I. A. Richards, Cleanth Brooks, and William Empson have pushed these partial, and extremely valuable, views to the limit. But ironic or ambiguous structures are merely special varieties of dialectical structures [. . .] I have tried to avoid the mistake of saying poetry, or good poetry, or the best poetry, is always dialectical; and it seems to me a worse and narrower mistake to say or to imply that poetry or good poetry or the best poetry is always ironic. (704–05)

Jarrell's criticism—and poetic practice—was informed by a theory much more dialectical than that of his New Critical mentors John Crowe Ransom, Cleanth Brooks, and Allen Tate. Take, for example, Jarrell's poem "A Quilt Pattern." This piece concerns a young boy who is negotiating psychological crisis through a dream. As in "A Sick Child," the child protagonist of this poem has been home all day, confined to bed:

> The blocked-out Tree
> Of the boy's Life is gray
> On the tangled quilt: the long day
> Dies at last, after many tales. (1–4)

The day dies; night approaches; twilight grays his quilt. His mother—there is no father in the poem—has been reading him fairy tales all day, the tales, particularly "Hansel and Gretel," providing a narrative pattern through which he can make sense out of what Jarrell suggests is the boy's unresolved Oedipal desire. He falls asleep, "falls / Through darkness [. . .] / Into the oldest story of all" (8–10), presumably the story of Eden, the story of innocence lost, the story of family romance. In "Levels and Opposites" Jarrell likens the process of reading a poem to that of a snowball rolling down a hillside: "most of the snow clings only for a moment and is thrown off, but some keeps rolling, more is added constantly, and quite a respectable snowball (or total impression) arrives at the bottom of the hill" (697). "A Quilt Pattern" operates in this fashion. Rather than striving for a tightly unified poem, Jarrell crafts a poem of *impressions,* a surreal dream sequence that complicates the already fragmented identity of the child.

The child is divided into "good me," "bad me," and "the Other," which Jarrell writes is analogous to the "Id" (*Letters* 303). The child's identity is complicated by his relationship to his mother. In the dream the child's mother is the edible house of "Hansel and Gretel," a source of childhood desire. The boy is the morphologically similar "mouse," who "breaks a finger / From the window and lifts it to his—" (45–46). This phrase, with its omitted word—perhaps "mouth," suggesting desire—is echoed later in the lines, in which "mother" is omitted:

> The taste of the house
> Is the taste of his— (58–59)

Mouth and mother are lashed together in syntactic and semantic structures. Just as the word *other* recalls *mother*, the id recalls its forbidden desire. At the climax of the poem it is the "Other" that finally thrusts the mother into the oven, in a scene fraught with sexual imagery and disturbing impressions:

> [The house] whispers, "you are full now, mouse—
> Look, I have warmed the oven, kneaded the dough:
> Creep in, ah, ah, it is warm!—
> Quick, we can slip the bread in now," says the house.
> He whispers, "I do not know
> How I am to do it."
>   "Goose, goose," cries the house,
> "It is big enough—just look!
> See if I bend a little, so—" (63–71)

Richard Flynn suggests that the relationship between the mother and child is abusive. He recalls Parker Tyler's argument that the poem's title is a pun on "*guilt*-pattern" (Flynn, *Randall Jarrell* 143), maintaining that the boy believes that "his Oedipal wish has been realized"—he has no father—and feels guilty (certainly conflicted) about his relationship with his mother (55). Certainly *something* has happened to the boy. He dreams: "My mother is basting / Bad me in the bath-tub / / [. . .] A Washcloth is turned like a mop in his mouth" (38–41). However, whether it is sexual abuse or, as Suzanne Ferguson argues, the boy feeling "imprisoned by [the mother's] solicitousness" (128) is debatable. Indeed, of the poem, Jarrell writes, "if I made a dream that could be interpreted, plainly, in only one possible way, that would be the undreamiest of dreams" (*Letters* 304). In short, the poem is anything but the "limp, static, entirely lifeless, [and] nevertheless [. . .] beautifully unified" poems he critiques in "Levels and Opposites." The poem is dialectical, contradictory. It is a snowball rolling down the hillside.

Yet there is no doubt that "A Quilt Pattern" is a well-crafted poem, one that utilizes dialectical structure to create "a system of developing tensions, of opposites struggling against each other" (Jarrell, "Levels" 702). The female speaker of Jarrell's "Seele im Raum" also speaks of struggling opposites. Cured of her delusions, she maintains that there is a difference between the "skin of being" that "owns [and] is owned / In honor or dishonor, that is borne and bears—" and "that raw thing, the being inside it / That has neither a wife, a husband, nor a child" (63–66). In *The Raw and the Cooked* Claude Levi-Strauss makes a point that resonates with the housewife's, positing that "the conjunction of a member of the social group with nature must be mediatized through the intervention of cooking fire, whose normal function is to mediatize the conjunction of the raw product and the human consumer, and whose operation thus has the effect of making sure that a natural creature is at one and the same time *cooked and socialized*" (336). We have an opposition between the natural "raw"—that which is not part of society, not acculturated, that which has "neither a wife, a husband, nor a child"—and that cooked "skin" that "owns, is owned," that is "*cooked and socialized*." This opposition is at the heart of the raw/cooked debate of the late '50s and early '60s and has been made analogous to form and content, subject and craftsmanship. Craftsmanship had no stronger advocate than Randall Jarrell. Writing of Gregory Corso, Jarrell makes clear his belief that poetry demands craftsmanship, that some degree of "cooking" is required, that Corso's first-thought-best-thought mentality would never facilitate great poetry: "Failure to select, exclude, compress, or aim toward a work of art [. . .] makes it impossible for even a talented beatnik [i.e., Corso] to write a good poem except by accident" (*Letters* 418).

Jarrell's use of form and regiment, his tendency to "select, exclude, compress," and to "cook" his poetry makes a good deal of sense in light of Levi-Strauss. The ingredients for Jarrell's poetry are natural ones, emotional ones—perhaps, at times, sentimental ones. Robert Lowell writes that *The Lost World* (1965), Jarrell's last book of poetry, concerns "solitude, the solitude of the unmarried, the solitude of the married, the love, strife, dependency, the indifference of man and woman—how mortals age, and brood over their lost and raw childhood, only recapturable in memory and imagination. Above all, childhood!" ("Randall Jarrell" 109). The forms and structures Jarrell employs act as the "cooking fire" that mediates the conjunction of these "raw" themes (the "raw product" in Levi-Strauss's terms) and the reader (the "human consumer"). In his self-dialogue, written as a tribute to Jarrell, James Dickey has his "A" persona rightly recognize that the "real" world is Jarrell's rather raw subject. He says, "[Jarrell] writes about things we know; that is, he writes about cats, common soldiers, about the dilemmas of children, and . . . and the small man, the man 'things are done to'" (36). Yet his "B" persona replies, "But these are *poems* he is trying to write. If you ignore that, you substitute sentimentality and special pleading [. . .] for the poet's true work" (39). The dichotomy between raw subject and cooked structure is one that preoccupied Jarrell throughout his career. Yet he most openly confronts this dichotomy in *The Bat-Poet,* his second children's book, the work that, in the words of Mary Jarrell, "triggered" *The Lost World* (*Remembering* 123), what Robert Lowell called "his last and best book" ("Randall Jarrell" 109).

Many critics have argued that the predominant mode of poetry written in contemporary North America is the scenic mode, also referred to as the poetics of "voice," or the poetry of "official verse culture."[7] Though the voice poem does not dominate the world of American children's poetry as it does for adults, it is certainly predominant in the world of official school poetry that is exemplified by Frost.[8] Jarrell, undoubtedly a member of the literary establishment, is often uncritically married to this poetics of voice, to the scenic mode of poetry, a mode that evokes the liberal humanist tradition by implying a coherent, whole, and self-knowing author, or, perhaps better, a "lyric speaker." This mode disguises the conflicting, unconscious, and socially contingent self of the author that is posited by postmodern theories, while simultaneously disguising the artificiality of the poet's language. Competing modes of poetry—say, those of nonsense verse and visual poetries (as we shall see in chapters 4 and 5)—foreground their artificiality. However, the scenic mode, it has been argued, disguises what might be called its more "cooked" elements. It strives to sound "natural," when the "natural" voice it achieves is in fact a highly tooled and revised linguistic artifact. As Charles Altieri argues in *Self and Sensibility in Contemporary American Poetry,* "[T]he desire [in the dominant mode] for sincerity or naturalness, for poetry as communication, seems continually in tension with the highly artificial means required to produce the desired effects at the level of intensity adequate for lyric poetry" (15). In *Poetry as Discourse* Antony Easthope anticipates Altieri's thesis, arguing convincingly that the dominant mode of poetry, particularly that revolving around the pentameter so disparaged by Koch and his fellows, works to disguise its constructedness by evoking a "proper" poetic voice, a "class dialect" (69). This dialect, he argues, "preclude[s] shouting and 'improper' excitement," the very elements so common in the lyrics of Allen Ginsberg and other Beats (69). Instead of the excited yawp of the Beats, the dialect "enhances the poise of a moderate yet uplifted tone of voice, an individual voice self-possessed, self-controlled, impersonally self-expressive" (69).[9] One has but to peruse any recent issue of *Poetry* to hear this "self-possessed" voice expressed, even if the line that speaks it is not pentameter. This mode is the poetry primarily of the cooked scene, the poetry lampooned by Koch, the poetry critiqued by the Language poets. In children's poetry one might turn for examples of this poetic to Myra Cohn Livingston, David McCord, or any number of voice poets. Jarrell's poetic is certainly highly structured with decidedly formalistic tendencies. Yet in contrast to, say, the sonnets of Richard Wilbur, whose early work exemplifies the cooked school, Jarrell's poems, especially those in *The Lost World,* do evince an extraordinary quality of what Mary Jarrell calls "conversational directness" (*Remembering* 121), though they are nowhere near the conversational quality of a Ginsberg or Frank O'Hara. Jarrell's work resists both sides of the binary, and his poems often reject the "self-possessed" voice so commonly found in the work of Wilbur and his acolytes, depicting selves that are incoherent and divided, selves in crisis like the housewife of "Seele im Raum" or the child of "A Quilt Pattern."

Though childhood had always played a part in Jarrell's poetry (Lowell called Jarrell "child Randall"), it was not until he was hospitalized for hepatitis in 1962 that Jarrell began writing *for* children. Spurred on by new Macmillan employee Michael di Capua, Jarrell began translating the brothers Grimm. Jarrell had not been producing many poems during this period. In fact, during the early '50s Jarrell had been writing mostly prose, including *Pictures from an Institution* (1954) and *Poetry and the Age* (1953). It seems he found his work on the Grimms' translations therapeutic. Once Jarrell regained his health, di Capua invited him and his wife to New York to discuss further projects. Mary recalls, "Jarrell was saying ruefully what a long time it had been since he had written any poems and at that di Capua made his move. 'What about writing for children, Randall?' he asked so smoothly. 'Have you ever thought of that?' And Jarrell, the children's writer, was invented" (*Children's Books* 3). *The Gingerbread Rabbit* and *The Bat-Poet,* Jarrell's first two children's books, were both published in 1964, four years after the release of Allen's anthology. Illustrated by Garth Williams, *The Gingerbread Rabbit* was moderately successful, but it was his sophomore effort that proved Jarrell's mettle as a children's book writer. In an interview with Aaron Kramer, Jarrell claimed that *The Gingerbread Rabbit* "wasn't a 'real' book" (qtd. in Mary Jarrell, *Remembering* 95). Rather, it seemed to be an exercise that Mary characterizes as something "a master chef cooks up [. . .] for his child on a day off" (96). She concludes, "It did not feel like a 'real' book [to Jarrell,] because in his innocence of the genre Randall had underrated it" (95–96). He lost this innocence by the time he began crafting *The Bat-Poet,* a complex fairy tale that concerns Jarrell's two favorite subjects: childhood and poetry. As Flynn notes in *Randall Jarrell and the Lost World of Childhood,* the book deals with a unique, talented child (bat though he may be) who simultaneously wants to be exceptional and accepted. Flynn argues that Jarrell, who never had a stable family of his own, develops in his children's books a consistent theme: "the need for happy yet improbable families that do not exist in the real world but have to be invented" (102). Though this theme is certainly a primary focus of *The Bat-Poet*'s narrative, Jarrell is simultaneously working through his notion of poetics. *The Bat-Poet* is an explicit embodiment of the poetics theorized in "Levels and Opposites," an embodiment that Mary claims "triggered" *The Lost World* and broke the writer's block that kept him from writing poetry.

Jarrell's *The Bat-Poet* demonstrates some of the contradictions that are apparent when constructing poetry in the dominant mode discussed earlier. The narrative that frames the poems in *The Bat-Poet* provides an interesting occasion for scrutinizing complications in the poetics of voice, and the complications and contradictions inherent in ascribing to a binary logic. The bat skirts the line between conservative and experimental, between the cooked and the raw. The complexity of the bat becomes apparent at the story's beginning, when Jarrell demonstrates his peculiar conservatism:

> Toward the end of summer all the bats except the little brown one began sleeping in the barn. He missed them, and tried to get them to come back and sleep on the porch with him. "What do you want to sleep in the barn for?" he asked them.
>
> "We don't know. [. . .] What do you want to sleep on the porch for?"
>
> "It's where we always sleep," he said. (2)

The little bat's longing for familiarity is apparent. He does not want to violate what has "always" been; he wants to maintain familiar customs. The other bats cannot offer any reason for their relocation, so our little hero, despite his loneliness, stays on the porch, for as he says, "If I slept in the barn I'd be homesick" (2). Paradoxically, it is his desire to maintain tradition that leads him to violate custom in a much more startling way.[10]

Before, sleeping amid the furry group of bats, the little bat would wake up during the day and immediately "push [. . .] himself up into the middle of them and go [. . .] right back to sleep" (2). However, now, alone on the porch, he does not go back to sleep; rather, he "just hang[s] there and think[s]" (2). Recalling Plato's allegory of the cave, the new world of daylight inspires the bat—but it is the mockingbird who introduces the bat to the world of poetry. The bat's emergence from night into the world of daylight—the waking world we all know—is much like the emergence of the dreamer into reality. In "The Death of the Ball Turret Gunner," for example, the unnamed gunner wakes "to the black flak and the nightmare fighters," just as Travisano notes that the speaker of "Next Day" "wakes into realities of loneliness, aging and earth that, until now, she has managed to 'overlook'" (*Midcentury* 62). However, the bat's lot is not nearly as bleak as that

27

of Jarrell's gunner and housewife. As Mary writes in *Remembering Randall,* Jarrell's children's books set their heroes "on the road marked Happy Ending" (96). Rather than waking, in that horrifying paradox, "to the nightmare fighters," Jarrell's bat wakes instead to a world of "green-and-gold-and-blue" (5). Unlike the child in "A Quilt Pattern," who falls into a black nightmare after "the long day / Dies" (3–4), the bat emerges into the bright light of day, a world filled with the mockingbird's song.

The bat realizes that he can never sing like the mockingbird (he hasn't the range), and so begins making up poems, understanding that "If you get the words right you don't need a tune" (5). The bat's respect for the mockingbird recalls Jarrell's respect for Robert Frost. During an encounter with Allen Ginsberg, Lawrence Ferlinghetti, and William Burroughs, Jarrell was asked to "demonstrate 'excellence' in poetry." Jarrell recited "Home Burial" (*Letters* 418).[11] As Frost's work did for Jarrell, the mockingbird's songs represent "excellence in poetry" for the little bat. In "The Group of Two" Mary writes, "In Life, Frost and Cal [Robert Lowell] were Mockingbirds . . . Bob Watson and Randall were Bats" (290). Frost and Lowell are closely tied to the cooked school of poets. Hall's first edition of *New Poets of England and America* featured an introduction by Frost, as well as thirteen pages of Lowell's verse. As we have seen in chapter 1, Frost referred to both Lowell and Donald Hall as "his children" whom he "helped bring up." In *The Children's Books of Randall Jarrell,* Jerome Griswold notes that "the resemblance between Frost and the mockingbird is unmistakable to those familiar with Frost's personality and idiosyncrasies" (56). Moreover, Griswold observes that Jarrell gave the mockingbird "Frost's peremptory and authoritative way which abashed younger poets, [and] his affectation of adopting a studied pose when listening" (56).

In his interview with Kramer, Jarrell says, though the "mockingbird is pretty bad [. . .] he's a *real* artist" (qtd. in Griswold 57). Unlike the Beats, who Jarrell claims can only "write a good poem [. . .] by accident," the mockingbird understands the craft of poetry (*Letters* 418). Unfortunately, Jarrell does not transcribe any of the mockingbird's songs; we hear only the poetry of his little protégé. Jarrell aligns the bat-poet against the mockingbird, giving the bat only an intuitive understanding of poetic form. Yet the bat's first fragment of poetry displays a tendency for the formal "cooked" verse of Hall's anthology:

> At dawn, the sun shines like a million moons
> And all the shadows are as bright as moonlight.
> The birds begin to sing with all their might.
> The world awakens and forgets the night.

The black-and-gray turns green-and-gold-and-blue.
The squirrels begin to— (1–6)

Although unfinished, we can see a highly structured and formally intricate pattern emerge from the lines. The poem's organization revolves around quatrains of iambic pentameter, which feature an unrhymed first line and a triplet following. Also, the last word of the first line, "moons," echoes with "blue" of the fifth line. The fragmented, five-syllable sixth line chimes perfectly with "blue," giving the poem formal closure even though it is contrived to be a fragment: "blue" and "begin to." The poem is formally complex in other ways as well. The triplet rhyme is subtle, the unaccented second syllable of "moonlight" downplays the couplet that follows and adds strength to the internal rhyme "bright" in line 2. Yet the narrative that surrounds the poem suggests that the bat is unaware of his technical prowess, that the bat's poetry is "natural," not artificial. Most voice-lyrics strive for such "natural" poetry that disguises its artificiality. In this case, Jarrell even has his bat resent any admiration of his ability at formal versification.

Because his fellow bats did not enjoy this first fragment, the bat moves on to different audiences, writing a new poem and reciting it for the mockingbird. Jarrell included this next poem in his final book of poetry, *The Lost World,* calling it "The Bird of Night." Untitled in *The Bat-Poet,* the poem begins by describing the owl as a silent "shadow [. . .] floating through the moonlight" (1). This shadow is an ominous one, however: "its claws are long, its beak is bright. / Its eyes try all the corners of the night" (3–4). As Perry Nodelman notes in his cursory reading of the poem in *The Pleasures of Children's Literature,* the piece "encourages us to think about the relationships of sound waves and waves of water; about the possibility of drowning and the possibility of death; [. . .] about the stillness of death and the act of keeping still in order to prevent death" (207):

> [. . .] all the air swells and heaves
> And washes up and down like water.
> The ear that listens to the owl believes
> In death. The bat beneath the eaves,
>
> The mouse beside the stone are still as death—
> The owl's air washes them like water. (5–10)

"The Bird of Night" tackles the idea of death, of being preyed upon, taking the point of view of smaller, weaker creatures—creatures that are much like children. On the metaphoric level, the owl becomes "the capricious infinite / That, like parents, no one has yet escaped / Except by luck or magic" that Jarrell writes of in "Children Selecting Books in a Library" (14–16). On the formal level the poem is a marvelous example of craft, of the bat-poet's ability "to select, exclude, compress, [and] aim toward a work of art" (Jarrell, *Letters* 408). It also subtly shows the bat's evolution as a poet. In "The Bird of Night" the bat uses formal structures similar to his first work. The poem is composed in loose iambic quatrains, the first stanza using the same rhymes found in "At Dawn the Sun Shines Like a Million Moons": "moonlight," "bright," and "night." Also, we see the bat again working with triplets, yet in this poem, the bat—unconsciously, of course—realizes that the rhymes may become overwhelming, so he inserts an unrhymed line between the first and second line of each triplet, enjambs the rhyme in the second stanza, and incorporates an interesting slant/sight rhyme in the last quatrain that calls attention to the theme of the poem: "death," "night," and "breath."

The mockingbird, "cooked" craftsman that he is, notices the formal beauty of the poem, saying, "Why, I like it. [. . .] Technically it's quite accomplished. The way you change the rhyme-scheme's particularly effective" (14). It is here that we realize the bat-poet composes these poems in ignorance: he responds, "It is?" And when the mockingbird acknowledges the "clever[ness]" of having "that last line two feet short," the bat is dumbfounded—he does not know meter. Jarrell, however, does. It is in the bat's exchange with the mockingbird that we encounter a rather interesting tension in Jarrell's poetic. Obviously, we are supposed to sympathize with the bat, the hero of the story. The mockingbird, pompous and self-important, understands craft on an intellectual level. He notices the very traits that Jarrell, in "Levels and Opposites," rejects as relatively unimportant: "metre, stanza form, rhyme, alliteration, quantity, and so on" (697). Thus, in his theorization of poetry, Jarrell "neglects these without too much regret: criticism has paid them an altogether disproportionate amount of attention—partly, I suppose, because they are things any child can point at, draw diagrams of, and count" (697). The bat, who functions as the child of *The Bat-Poet,* cannot "point at, draw diagrams of, and count" these formal traits—he does not realize he is employing them. The mockingbird, however, does. He correctly notes that the shortened final line gives "the effect of the night holding its breath," and he explains the effect in terms of the poem's interesting metrical and syllabic variations, whereas the bat maintains he "just made it like holding your breath" (14). In fact, the bat, upset at the analytical mockingbird, later fumes, "Why, I might as well have said it to the bats. What do I care how many feet it has? The owl nearly kills me, and he says he likes the rhyme-scheme!" (15). The tension lies in the fact that Jarrell, the actual composer of "The Bird of Night," understands how the poem works formally, and most probably—perhaps most certainly—composed the verse with the formal structures in mind. The two characters represent the two competing schools of poetry and perhaps the two sides of Jarrell's poetic—the bat approximating the raw, and the mockingbird suggesting the cooked.

In the chipmunk the bat finds an audience who responds to his poetry emotionally rather than intellectually, to the content rather than the form. After hearing "The Bird of Night," the chipmunk "gave a big shiver and said, 'it's terrible, just terrible! Is there really something like that at night?'" (17). The bat is pleased by this response and later reflects, "*He* didn't say any of that two-feet-short stuff [. . .] *he* was scared!" (19). The bat writes his newfound friend a poem, "The Chipmunk's Day," a poem that is situated between the two poles of formal verse and free verse. Prefiguring his final poem, "Bats," "The Chipmunk's Day" appears rather loose in construction. This five-stanza piece begins with a perfect line of trochaic pentameter, though it vacillates between iambic and trochaic meter—sometimes losing its metrical feel altogether:

> In and out the bushes, up the ivy,
> Into the hole
> By the old stump, the chipmunk flashes.
> Up the pole
>
> To the feeder full of seeds he dashes,
> Stuffs his cheeks,
> The chickadee and titmouse scold him.
> Down he streaks. (*Bat-Poet* 20)

The lines begin with a fairly regular syllabic pattern, but the pattern is varied to such a degree that the exception becomes the rule. The second line of the first stanza is iambic dimeter, while the second line of the second stanza is an amphimacer, or perhaps another line of iambic dimeter beginning with a headless iamb. But when we get to the third stanza—its second line being "Red as a fox"—we realize that an exact, regular meter is not the goal; rather, the goal is a living, heard rhythm, one that is rooted in traditional prosody, but not enslaved by it. Furthermore, while the poem does rhyme, the rhymes occur only in the second and fourth line of each stanza. Yet form mirrors content, for the poem's peculiar mix of long and short lines and their varied placement echoes the subject—the harried and quick chipmunk. The chipmunk recognizes this fact, remarking, "It goes all in and out, doesn't it?" (22).

The next poem in the book speaks directly of the mockingbird. Untitled in *The Bat-Poet*, Jarrell placed it second in *The Lost World* and titled it, simply, "The Mockingbird."[12] The poem at once exalts the bird and deprecates it. In this poem too the bat works with triple rhymes, employing an ABAABCD rhyme scheme throughout (the possible slant rhyme "rising" and "soaring" occurs only in the first stanza). The meter is loose, and the lines vary between nine and thirteen syllables. But the poem's loose form gives it the organic quality Jarrell so desired in his poetry:

> Look one way and the sun is going down,
> Look the other and the moon is rising.
> The sparrow's shadow's longer than the lawn.
> The bats squeak: "Night is here," the birds cheep: "Day is gone."
> On the willow's highest branch, monopolizing
> Day and night, cheeping, squeaking, soaring,
> The mockingbird is imitating life. (*Bat-Poet* 28)

The rhymes are not forced, and the bat uses slant rhymes to good effect, rhyming "down" with "lawn;" "yard" with "bird." Many of the rhymes are enjambed, affording them a quiet power not heard in his first fragmented poem. But ultimately it is the content that makes the poem stand out. We watch the tension hinted at in the first two lines—the tension between the rising moon and the setting sun—develop throughout the poem, suggesting the binary opposition of *and* the liminal space between night and day, imitation and reality, truth and fiction, nature and artifice. After a list of the many creatures the mockingbird/poet can imitate, the final stanza (including the telling rhyme "sing" and "anything") ends with a question:

> Now, in the moonlight, he sits here and sings.
> A thrush is singing, then a thrasher, then a jay—
> Then, all at once, a cat begins meowing.
> A mockingbird can sound like anything.
> He imitates the world he drove away
> So well that for a minute, in the moonlight,
> Which one's the mockingbird? which one's the world? (*Bat-Poet* 28)

This question resonates with the poem's form, for the poem is about poetry—about the power of words to imitate life. And the form of the poem appears organic, pliable, living.

Speaking of poets and mockingbirds, Jarrell once said:

> I've known a lot of artists and poets . . . and . . . I write poetry myself—or
> anyway, I write verse myself. . . . Several times when I've talked with writer
> friends about this book I'm amused to see how they immediately identify
> with the mockingbird. (Laugh) But the hero of the book is a bat who is really
> quite nice. [. . .] Territoriality at its strongest is in mockingbirds . . . (pause)
> So, it seemed to me that . . . mockingbirds are not only more like artists than
> other birds, they're more like people too. (qtd. in Griswold 57–58)

Griswold sees this statement as one that is cautiously criticizing Frost
"through Jarrell's gambit of acknowledging the same faults in himself" (58).
Jarrell's interviewer asks Jarrell about this "territoriality," saying, "Well,
you're certainly not that kind of poet, Jarrell" (58). Jarrell answers, "Oh . . .
but . . . but if I'm not . . . I'm not a poet, I'm afraid. I mean . . . I mean . . .
(Laugh)" (58). The mockingbird, then, brings to the surface some of Jarrell's
deep-rooted concerns about poetry, and perhaps concerns about his own
poetic. Jarrell says, "I write poetry myself—or anyway, I write verse myself"
(57). This distinction between verse and poetry is an important one. In
Rhyme's Reason John Hollander makes a similar distinction: "Poetry is a mat-
ter of trope; and verse, of scheme and design [. . .] which is why most verse
is not poetry" (1). The mockingbird, representing the cooked, acculturated,
formal poets, drives out life to imitate it, and his poetry, as Flynn speculates,
is "mostly artifice" (109). However, the bat seeks to join with the life he
writes about—he wants to be accepted by a society, a family—the family,
perhaps, that Jarrell never had. As Flynn writes, Jarrell "dissociated himself
from those he loved the most because he feared losing them" (*Randall Jar-
rell* 3). He continues, noting that Jarrell's childhood was complicated by the
divorce of his parents and the resultant—and for Jarrell, too-brief—move
to his grandparents' home in Hollywood. Flynn maintains that this "abrupt
separation from [his grandparents], combined with the onset of adolescence
and the pain of his parents' divorce [. . .] created a sense of betrayal" in the
young Randall (4). If, as Mary remembers, Jarrell believed that his "family
[was] a disaster" (qtd. in Flynn 3), then *The Bat-Poet* makes clear both Jar-
rell's and the bat's ultimate desire to be accepted by a family, an acceptance
predicated on poetic knowledge. Poetry, for Jarrell and his bat, must imitate
life without killing it—without driving it away.

But as we have seen, the bat's poetry does not reflect the completely
raw verse of the Beats and New York school poets. Rather, *The Bat-Poet* re-
veals a complicated, postmodern poetic, one that rejects easy binaries and
embraces contradiction. The bat's compositional process mirrors the raw
school, but his product is formal, if only accidentally. In "Levels and Op-

posites" Jarrell writes, "A poem is made inexhaustible like a thing, an organism, a perception, instead of exhaustible like a generalization, primarily by means of the many dialectical contradictory relationships I have mentioned—structural ones are particularly important" (703). In this respect *The Bat-Poet* as story is quite a lot like a poem, for it suggests "[t]he generalizations most akin to poetry" that Jarrell outlines in "Levels and Opposites," those that "tend to be paradoxical, contradictory, ambiguous, in form as well as in content" (703). For instance, the bat's poems are not formal by design, for the bat is ignorant of the forms he employs, yet they do display the conventions of formal verse: rhyme and meter. Jarrell crafts the bat as representing the individual, natural genius, one who practically invents poetry because of his inability to sing like the mockingbird, for "his high notes were all high, and his low notes were all high and the notes in between were all high" (5). Though he models his poems throughout the book on the mockingbird's song lyrics, the bat is intuiting conventions without realizing that they are part of a larger, socially contingent discourse of poetry, a discourse that Jarrell—like Koch and indeed all the poets in Donald Allen's anthology—studied quite closely. Jarrell's bat is not implicated in the paradox that Koch is caught up in: the rejection of tradition while remaining steeped and informed by it. However, Jarrell is not the bat, and Jarrell as cultural critic and poet revels in the fact that he is steeped in and informed by tradition. Initially it seems Jarrell either assumes that children are not ready to understand what makes Jarrell the kind of poet he is, or he is unaware of the socially constructed nature of himself and of poetry.

For example, the bat says, "The trouble isn't making poems, the trouble's finding somebody that will listen to them" (15). However, Jarrell's own experience with composing verse was quite different from the bat's. Jarrell had been writing few poems during the early '50s and continued to write poems only in spurts throughout the remainder of the decade, sometimes going *years* without completing a draft. Mary Jarrell notes his completion of "In Montecito" in 1960 as being "his first poem in two years," and in his National Book Award acceptance speech Jarrell himself admits, "Sometimes a poem comes to me—I do what I can to it when it comes—and sometimes for years not one comes" (*Letters* 445, 448). Of course, we should not disparage Jarrell for writing a fantasy instead of an autobiography, but it seems worthwhile to note that his book reinforces for child readers problematic notions of individual genius. Yet we must not forget that though the bat claims, "The trouble isn't making poems," he nevertheless has a bout of writer's block later in the book. The bat finds himself unable to craft a poem about the cardinal, despite his promise to do so:[13] "But it was no use: no matter how much the bat watched, he never got an idea [for a poem]. Finally he went to the chipmunk and said in a perplexed voice: 'I can't make up a poem about the cardinal. [. . .] I don't know why I can't, but I can't. I watch him and he's just beautiful, he'd make a beautiful poem; but I can't think of anything'" (25). The scene highlights the painstaking level of observation necessary (though, Jarrell suggests, not always sufficient) to compose poetry. The bat observes the cardinal, noting the odd "way [he] cracked the sunflower seeds; instead of standing on them and hammering them open, like a titmouse, he'd turn them over and over in his beak—it gave him a thoughtful look—and all at once the seed would fall open, split in two" (24).

We can read this image as a metaphor for reading poems, turning them "over and over" in one's mind rather than hammering at them "like a titmouse." However, we can also read it as a suggestion of the difficulty of writing poetry, of treating subjects, of turning experience into poetry. We can read it as a comment on the "thoughtful" activity involved in crafting poems. Here the bat is no first-thought-best-thought O'Hara, hammering out poems on his lunch break. Unlike the poets presented in Allen's anthology, Jarrell resists the romantic construction of the poet as a genius whose first thought is the best thought, while showing the limitations that poets— like himself, like the bat—can encounter when treating diverse subjects, even the most compelling subjects. The book embraces the dialectic theory outlined in "Levels and Opposites," setting against each other irreconcilable tensions, tensions that are not working toward "a simple unity" but that operate in a more heterogeneous manner, accentuating "opposing forces" (699).

Another of these tensions lies in the fact that despite Griswold's insistence that the mockingbird represents Frost, elements of Jarrell are found in both the bat and the mockingbird. In *Remembering Randall,* Mary suggests, "'The Mockingbird' is a caricature drawn from Randall's knowledge of Lowell's and Frost's, *and his own,* self-obsession, acute sensitivity, and fierce territoriality" (103). Certainly, Jarrell sounds more than a little like the mockingbird in his reviews. For example, in a 1950 omnibus review Jarrell turns his critical eye to Elizabeth Coatsworth's *The Creaking Stair,* a collection of children's poems. His response is rather tepid, yet Jarrell finds occasion to compliment Coatsworth's line *"skimming the broth or pouring that thick tea"* in mockingbird fashion: "The extra foot in the last line—no other line in the poem has five—helps to make *that thick tea* a triumph" ("Poetry" 158). However, in the same review, after proclaiming that "There isn't a good poem" in Louis Simpson's new book, Jarrell advises the poet, "Whatever you do, don't pay any attention to critics" (157). Jarrell's review of John Ciardi's *As If* (a collection for adults) further complicates Jarrell's status as a mockingbird figure. In this review Jarrell finds fault with Ciardi's tendency to copy—to mock—other poets. He writes, "[Ciardi] uses Steven's, or Shapiro's, or half a dozen other poets' tricks and techniques as easily, and with as much justification, as a salesman would use a competitor's sales talk—it works, doesn't it?" (26).

At times, then, the bat seems like one of these new poets, tutored and critiqued by a Jarrell-like critic. Jarrell's advice to Simpson applies equally well to the bat: "Mr. Simpson seems genuinely wild: sometimes he sounds like himself, a surprising creature in a surprising world" ("Poetry" 157). And this "surprising creature" is a poet who grows and changes, who apparently is learning—even if intuitively—new methods for crafting verse, new subjects for treatment. His final poem, "Bats," which also appears in *The Lost World,* is the most like free verse of all the bat's poems, and in it the bat—that "surprising creature"—"sounds like himself," for he learns to write of himself, of his own kind. Flynn notes that the bat-poet "taps [childhood's] poetic resources and through the mature, articulate means of the adult artist, transforms them into poetry" (*Randall Jarrell* 109). The narrator tells us that the bat found this poem "easier [to write] than the other poems, somehow: all he had to do was remember what [childhood] had been like and every once in a while put in a rhyme" (35). "Bats," then, exemplifies Jarrell's brief comments on rhyme that preface his work in John Ciardi's *Mid-Century American Poets* (1950): "Rhyme as an automatic structural device, automatically attended to, is attractive to me, but I like it best irregular, live, and heard" (183). The bat moves from the rhymed triplets in his first fragment, to the irregularly rhymed "The Chipmunk's Day," and finally to the "automatic [. . .] irregular, live, and heard" rhymes that are present in "Bats," the bat-poet's best work, rife with internal oppositions.

The bat's first fragment is formally perfect: its triplets are aligned neatly; its last, truncated line still rhymes despite its premature end. Yet it is in "Bats" that we find evidenced the contradictions in structure and content that Jarrell argued made for great poetry. Structurally the bat's rhymes are unobtrusive, establishing no consistent pattern. The line breaks are dictated by the integrity of the line and not by predetermined formal structures. The first line is iambic dimeter, "A bat is born," and stands in contrast with the variant rhythms of the second, "Naked and blind and pale." The rhythmic strength of the line lies in the accented first syllable followed by two unstressed syllables. The final two iambs lead smoothly into the next line, where we hear the first rhyme. Yet the rhyme is enjambed, subduing the perfect, accented rhyme of "pale" and "tail." In fact, the first three lines are a broken couplet: "A bat is born / Naked and blind and pale" form the first hidden line of pentameter; "His mother makes a pocket of her tail" forms the next. However, the bat is not interested in the conventions of heroic verse, so from the beginning the form is broken—at least on the page—just as the first line of pentameter is broken. Perhaps the bat would agree with Koch's sentiments, "farewell stale pale skunky pentameters."

The poem represents a dialectic between the raw and the cooked, in both its form and its content. The bat is "born / Naked and blind and pale"—raw, untouched by civilization and culture (1–2). The mother's body is the only clothing, the only protection he needs. The baby bat "clings to her long fur / By his thumbs and toes and teeth" as she "dances through the night" (4–6). In *The Raw and the Cooked* Levi-Strauss mentions some of the many idioms that inform the concept of the raw; two of them interestingly are *danser à cru* ("to dance raw") and *monter à cru* ("to ride bareback"), and both the young bat and his mother participate in these activities (335). In fact, the entirety of the poem participates in the world of the raw. As the chipmunk notes, the bats "sleep all day and fly all night [. . .] and eat while [they're] flying and drink while [they're] flying" (40). The only light comes from the distant stars and the heatless moon, and as day breaks the mother "folds her wings about her sleeping child" and joins him in repose. Yet the poem also participates in the world of the cooked. Though the bats eat their food raw and drink while "skim[ming] across" the water, the poem depicts a process of acculturation, a process that mirrors the process of cooking that Levi-Straus speaks of. Their midnight activities act "as a mediatory activity between heaven and earth, life and death, nature and culture" (65).

The bat's childhood has so thoroughly acculturated him that he still yearns for the company of his fellow bats just as Jarrell wished for a happy family. Though presently independent, the bat wants nothing more than to "snuggle [. . .] closer to the others," the very last words of the book (43). It is "Bats" that allows him to reenter the culture his daylight activities have estranged him from. It is a tool that facilitates his return, and once he enters the barn and finds his way into the throng of bats, he discovers he "couldn't remember the words" of his poem (43). Beginning to drift into hibernation with the others, the bat's only concern is "I wish I'd said we sleep all winter" (43). With that, he closes his eyes and falls asleep, surrounded by the warmth of his family. The bat is not a versifier, as Jarrell called himself; he is a poet. Yet despite Jarrell's self-deprecation—his insistence that he writes verse, not poetry—Jarrell too is a poet whose work, like the bat's (for the bat's work is his), embraces contradiction and opposition. *The Bat-Poet* implicitly encourages us to resist imagining poetry as merely technical prowess, as mere syllable counting. *The Bat-Poet* constructs poetry as a cultural artifact that *does something* in the world. Through poetry, the bat forges new relationships and comes, through poetic knowledge, to better understand himself and his place with the other bats. It is the bat's ability to resist Levi-Strauss's binaries—and the somewhat artificial binary suggested by Hall's and Allen's anthologies—that ultimately wins him what Jarrell desired more than anything else: acceptance by his family, a happy return home. It is *The Bat-Poet*'s similar resistance to these binaries that makes it such an insightful work of literature, an antidote to our proclivity to choose "camps" and draw poetic lines in the sand. In this respect *The Bat-Poet* is somewhat of a rare book, one teaching that opposing tendencies and internal contradictions make for interesting poetry, that poetry is more complex than the simple binaries of "raw" and "cooked."

3

Child Poets
and the Poetry of the Playground

Mine eyes have seen the glory of the burning of the school.
We have tortured every teacher, we have broken every rule.
We have thrown away our homework and we hanged the principal.
Our school is burning down.

Jim, St. Patrick's Parochial School
Bedford, New York
ca. 1960s

As many teachers know, Randall Jarrell's *The Bat-Poet* is not only a touching, sensitively rendered fairy tale. It is also a very effective—and commonly employed—introduction to both the reading and writing of poetry. As we've seen in chapter 2, *The Bat-Poet* suggests Jarrell's complex and dialectical theory of poetry, but it also touches on the competing impulses that might drive one to versify, the satisfying and unsatisfying reactions one's poetry might elicit, the social function of poetry, and even elements of craft. Although Jarrell's bat-poet is of uncertain age, it seems reasonable to read him as a child, or perhaps an adolescent. The bat-poet is a precocious student of poetry, and though he once enrages his mentor, the mockingbird, by writing a somewhat ambivalent piece about him, the bat nonetheless composes the "right" kind of poetry, the poetry of the schoolhouse, or what I call official school poetry. He is one of the rare students Kenneth Koch remembers initially desiring for his first Teachers and Writers workshop—that is, a child "who already like[s] poetry" ("Interview" 274). The bat writes poems of which poet and critic Myra Cohn Livingston would probably approve— "fine poetry" that exhibits phonological cohesion, that displays "the judicious use of rhythm, rhyme, assonance, alliteration, and other tools of the craft" (*Child as Poet* 22, 256). In short, the bat represents the good student, one who accepts and works within the traditions of adult poetry. Certainly there are human children who, like the bat, strive to emulate the adult poets they encounter, but more common are those raconteurs, as Iona Opie calls them, who specialize in the sometimes bawdy playground poetry. These child poets serve to remind us of what children often do with language while outside grown-up supervision. As we will see, they reveal that children have a poetic tradition of their own, a carnivalesque tradition that signifies on adult culture, even while producing poetry that rewards repeat listenings. I argue that any comprehensive study of American children's poetry—and, more broadly, poetry in general—is ultimately insufficient insofar as it fails to acknowledge and consider playground poetry as poetry, as belonging to a rich poetic tradition.[1]

Before addressing this tradition, we must first discuss "official school poetry," the dominant mode of children's poetry in the school, the kind of poetry written by adults and taught to children in the classroom. Charles Altieri writes, "A mode becomes dominant when it develops institutional power—both as a model for the ways in which agents represent themselves and, more important, as the basic example of what matters in reading and in attributing significance to what one reads" (8). No doubt official school poetry is dominant: championed in the schools and elevated in education textbooks, official school poetry—a *type* of poetry—has come to stand in for poetry *in its entirety,* both in the classroom and in literary criticism. As we've seen, Robert Frost exemplifies official school poetry; however, all poetry belonging to this group need not resemble Frost's work in theme or form. Rather, official school poetry is notable for its apparent teachability, its use of literary devices, its use of, in the words of Livingston, the "tools of the craft" (a phrase that makes poetry seem much more monolithic than it is). Frost's poetry is eminently teachable, emblematic of the "life and death commitment to authentic linguistic enactment" that James Applewhite writes of in "Poetry and Value" (473). Applewhite uses Frost's work as an example of the "achievements" that should be "set apart [. . .] from lesser, slacker users of poetic language" (473).

Poems selected for classroom use are principally the least politically and formally vexing; they appear easily thematizable and interpretable and thus are classroom friendly. Their classroom friendliness also lies in the fact that their politics is often difficult to excavate, even as they implicitly privilege the adult poetic tradition. Classroom practices (informed by problematic assumptions regarding poetic language) encourage misinformed readings of official school poems (most famously, the common notion that Frost's ultimately dark "The Road Not Taken" is an inspirational poem, a reading that hinges upon an almost willful inattention to language).

In *The American Poetry Wax Museum* Jed Rasula contends that poetry anthologies—and, by extension, current trends in poetry pedagogy—serve to turn otherwise exciting and powerful poetry into wax figures set upon a "waxen shrine" preserved for "an air-conditioned immortality" (2). He characterizes the wax museum mentality evidenced in the practice of anthologizing as a "carceral archipelago," writing that his aim, "in elaborating this thesis of a poetry wax museum, is to suggest that the seemingly autonomous 'voices and visions' of poets themselves have been underwritten by custodial sponsors who have surreptitiously turned down the volume on certain voices, and simulated a voice-over for certain others. Nothing defines the situation more succinctly than the police phrase *protective custody*" (33). Though he is discussing the canon of contemporary American poetry for adults, a stronger argument could be made for official school poetry for children. The custodians in this respect are the teachers, the adults who are needed to understand, to interpret, and indeed to produce poetry, whereas the museums are school-approved textbooks and anthologies. Rasula reminds us of Michel de Certeau, who in *The Practice of Everyday Life* maintains, in Rasula's paraphrase, "The dominant modern institutions [. . .] are colonization, psychiatry, and pedagogy, which focus and bring into line the renegade tendencies of the masses, the unconscious, *and the child*" (31, my emphasis). Calling American poetry a "social 'imaginary,'" Rasula laments that "poems have rarely circulated in America as cultural items, as *pragmata* of daily life. They appear, when they do, as exotic species, nurtured with devotion. So poems are not intrinsically distinct from museum specimens, curiosities in need of explanation, of reassuring placement" (31). This certainly is the case with official school poetry for children. Of course, this mode of poetry will always have a place in the classroom, where adults often have good reasons for teaching what they teach—but it is important to regard children's culture *alongside* adult culture. However, as I have suggested, the poetry emerging from the cultures of childhood is too often overlooked, deemed "lesser," "slacker," as Applewhite might say. This poetry is "turned down" and "voiced over" by official school poetry and the critical conversation surrounding it, and it does in fact exist as *pragmata* of the child's daily life, as a body of work that children use and manipulate, generally without adult intervention, "explanation," or "reassuring placement." This poetry is the poetry of the playground.

As its production is not monitored by authority figures, poetry of the playground is often vulgar, violent, and, I might add, uproariously funny: it embodies "the renegade tendencies of [. . .] the unconscious, and the child" that Rasula mentions (31). If official school poetry is a museum piece, archived in air-conditioned anthologies for students, then playground poetry is the graffiti on the museum walls, the notes penned on the anthology's cover. Its very nature makes it unlikely that playground poetry would be domesticated by being anthologized *for* children, as opposed to being collected by folklorists. (Iona and Peter Opie's *I Saw Esau: The Schoolchild's*

Pocket Book is a notable exception.)² From the point of view of most adults, playground poetry is uncanny. The poems are not "frightening," nor do they generate the "dread and horror" that Freud associates with *unheimlich* ("The 'Uncanny'" 339). However, in many ways they are "disturbing, suspect, [and] strange," all qualities that Anthony Vidler attributes to the uncanny (23). Vidler writes that the uncanny "might be characterized as the quintessential bourgeois kind of fear: one carefully bounded by the limits of real material security and the pleasure principle afforded by a terror that was, artistically at least, kept well under control" (4). This fear is the result of "a yet unfinished history that pits the homely, the domestic, the nostalgic, against their ever-threatening, always invading and often subversive 'opposites'" (13). Playground poetry operates as one of these subversive opposites. It dismantles nostalgic notions of the innocent, obedient, and controllable child and thus, in my experience, tends to disturb adults, as it implies sexualized, complicated child-agents who are able to control their world through linguistic play and sometimes violent, antiauthoritarian imagery.

Playground poetry, as an oral tradition, vexes privileging notions of the individual, authorial genius, while simultaneously complementing the adult, largely literary, poetic tradition(s). In *Poetry as Discourse* Antony Easthope argues, "Bourgeois poetic discourse now has no real audience" (161). He claims that most people, rather than turning to poetry, instead turn to "such genuinely contemporary media as cinema, television and popular song in its many varieties" (161). He may be right. But the poetry of the playground exists outside of the "bourgeois poetic discourse" Easthope discusses. It is folk-poetry, aligned with "nursery rhymes, the lore of schoolchildren, ballad, industrial folk song and even, more recently, the football chant" (65). The poetry of the playground exists in the space between original composition and received oral tradition. The poems are public property. Like the nursery rhymes of Mother Goose, no one child "owns" these poems; they belong to each child equally, and each child retains the right to alter and revise the poems as he or she sees fit, as context and mood dictates. There are no "great authors," white male or otherwise. Rather, there is a *community* of author/performers. As Iona Opie writes in *People in the Playground,* "The expression most likely to mislead an adult enquirer is 'I made it up.' To a child this is the direct equivalent of 'It came into my head' and has no connection with creativity. [. . .] The phrase 'I made it up' is so universal in this context that all doubts of juvenile honesty must be suppressed. Probably memory is the same as creation in a child's mind" (3–4). The authors are anonymous, yet the authors are everywhere.

In *Knock at a Star,* a popular poetry anthology for children, X. J. and Dorothy Kennedy quip, "After Shakespeare, Anonymous may be the second best poet in our language. At least, he or she wrote more good poems than most poets who sign what they write" (6). By pairing "Anonymous" with Shakespeare, the Kennedys elide the folk and communal nature of anonymous poetry, rewriting the oral, folk tradition in terms of literate traditions. The poem that inspires this comment, "Algy," while clever, certainly lacks the material force of many—if not most—of the American playground poems collected by folklorists in the last thirty years:

> Algy met a bear,
> The bear met Algy.
> The bear was bulgy,
> The bulge was Algy.

The other examples they give of "the second best poet in our language" are equally clever, though oddly nonrepresentative of the kinds of verse compiled in *Greasy Grimy Gopher Guts* or *One Potato, Two Potato*. Many of the poems collected in these texts similarly deal with death. However, they frequently do so much more graphically, employing startling, often upsetting imagery coupled with a great degree of rhythmic, musical play, though certainly they share with "Algy" the impulse to play with language on the morphological and syntactical level. Later in the book, the Kennedys provide an example of a jump-rope rhyme, asking child readers whether they can "write a new one," reminding them, "Don't forget to try it out on the playground," implicitly inscribing a distinction between verse appropriate for the classroom and verse appropriate for the playground:

> Teddy bear, teddy bear, turn around,
> Teddy bear, teddy bear, touch the ground,
> Teddy bear, teddy bear, show your shoe,
> Teddy bear, teddy bear, out go you! (151)

Francelia Butler includes this rhyme in *Skipping Around the World* (though without the inversion in the final line), and calls it "One of the best known of the action or agility rhymes" (119). It is odd that the Kennedys select this verse from all those available, because, as Butler reminds us, "Teddy Bear" is an agility rhyme, employed to provoke body movements and showcase jumping prowess rather than to flaunt wit and lyrical inventiveness.

If we compare "Teddy Bear" to the majority of the pieces included in Butler's *Skipping Around the World*, we suspect immediately that concerns about publishing holdups and parental reaction might have played a role in the Kennedys' selection. The Kennedys' choice avoids much of the spirit and many of the themes that predominate in playground rhyme, themes that recall Mikhail Bakhtin's theory of the carnivalesque. Bakhtin's theories have proved useful in the literary analysis of children's texts, because children's literature is often marked by what John Stephens has called "a playfulness which situates itself in positions of nonconformity" (121). He continues, noting that the carnivalesque in children's literature "expresses opposition to authoritarianism and seriousness, and is often manifested as parody of prevailing literary forms and genres, or as literature in non-canonical forms. Its discourse is often idiomatic, and rich in a play of signifiers" (121). Jon Scieszka and Lane Smith's *The Stinky Cheese Man and Other Fairly Stupid Tales* and Roald Dahl's *Revolting Rhymes* are perfect examples of this playful, carnivalesque literature. Joel Chaston has argued convincingly that L. Frank Baum's *Oz* books similarly embody Bakhtin's theories.[3] However, Stephens notes that though carnivalesque children's literature frequently

> mock[s] and challenge[s] authoritative figures and structures of the adult world—parents, teachers, political and religious institutions—and some of the (often traditionally male) values of society such as independence, individuality, and the activities of striving, aggression, and conquest, [it fails to] make extensive use of the abusive language or the insulting words or expression generally characteristic of the carnivalesque in its breaking of the norms of official speech. (122)

Stephens is correct when considering literature produced, published, and distributed by adults for children, but when we consider the oral traditions of children themselves, we see none of the hesitance to employ the language of the billingsgate evidenced in mainstream American children's literature.

Though *carnival* regularly serves a repressive function in society—a steam valve of sorts—the performance of playground poems circumvents this repressive function. As we will see, the poems do employ carnivalesque images and hierarchical inversion, but children generally chant them outside the purview of watchful adults. Most adults, especially those who monitor schoolyards (and my students testify to this), chastise and reprimand children for chanting the more obscene and obviously sexual rhymes. Unlike, say, Mardi Gras, which operates as a sanctioned "time-out" (without the punitive connotation that term has attracted for young people over the last decade or so), the recitation of playground poems—especially the very off-color rhymes—is rarely encouraged by adults (though exceptions do exist). Furthermore, these rhymes are not a once-a-year, strictly monitored release of tension. Of course, recess itself is a "time-out," but playground poetry is not chanted exclusively during recess. These poems exist as an ever-present fact in the life of most children, be they chanters or listeners. De Certeau is useful in explaining the function of playground poetry. Following Michel

Foucault's analysis of power in *Discipline and Punish,* de Certeau explores "how an entire society resists being reduced to [discipline, or, in French, *surveillance*]." He asks, "what popular procedures (also 'miniscule' and quotidian) manipulate the mechanism of discipline and conform to them only in order to evade them . . . ?" (xiv). I hold that playground poetry is one of these procedures, serving as one of "the clandestine forms taken by the dispersed, tactical, and makeshift creativity of groups or individuals[,]" like children, "already caught in the nets of 'discipline'" (xiv).

Take, for example, this jump-rope rhyme collected by Butler in New York City, a rhyme I remember chanting as a child:

> Abraham Lincoln
> Was a good old soul.
> He washed his face
> In a toilet bowl.
> He jumped out the window
> With his dick in his hand,
> And said, "'Scuse me, ladies!
> I'm superman."

Similarly, the two poems below, variants of the same motif, provide further examples of carnivalesque imagery and diction. Butler indicates that these two poems have been frequently chanted in U.S. playgrounds between 1965 and 1988, though there is no reason to doubt they are still chanted today:

> I fucked your mama
> Till she went blind.
> Her breath is bad
> But she sure can grind.

> I hate to talk about your mama;
> She's a good old soul.
> She's got a ten-ton pussy
> And a rubber ass-hole.[4]

The differences between the Kennedys' selection and the three rhymes above are manifest. Bakhtin's theories of carnival laughter are helpful in teasing out the implications of these differences. In *Rabelais and His World* Bakhtin argues that carnivalesque images "are opposed to all that is finished and polished, to all pomposity, to every ready made solution in the sphere of thought and world outlook" (3). The child poet implied by the Kennedys' selection is readily containable, is cute, is controllable by the adult: "Can you write a new one?" they ask the child, ordering, with an exclamation point, "Don't forget to try it out on the playground!" (151), to which we might add, "but not in the classroom!" The child poet/performer implied by the three rhymes above, however, is resistant, rebellious. The child does not need an adult's encouragement, and in fact the poems fly in the face of adult authority, be that adult a former chief executive of the United States or the even more powerful mother. The poet/performer recalls the folk implied by Bakhtin's *Rabelais,* the folk that Michael Holquist characterizes as "blasphemous rather than adoring, cunning rather than intelligent; they are coarse, dirty, and rampantly physical, reveling in oceans of strong drink, poods of sausage, and endless coupling of bodies" (xix).

Furthermore, the poems illustrate a recurring theme in playground poetry: they evince a fundamental tension between the body and the mind, a tension designed to produce either laughter or disgust, perhaps both. This laughter—festive laughter, Bakhtin would call it—is not "an individual reaction to some isolated 'comic' event" (11). Rather, it is "universal in scope; it is directed at all and everyone, including the carnival's participants" (11):

> Abraham Lincoln
> Was a good old soul.
> He washed his face
> In a toilet bowl.

These four lines exemplify grotesque realism, which Bakhtin argues works by pitting exaltation and debasement against each other: "Earth is an element that devours, swallows up (the grave, the womb) and at the same time an element of birth, of renascence (the maternal breasts). Such is the meaning of 'upward' and 'downward' in their cosmic aspect, while in their purely bodily aspect, which is not clearly distinct from the cosmic, the upper part is the face or the head and the lower part is the genital organs, the belly, and the buttocks" (21). Abraham Lincoln, a figure most American schoolchildren are taught to revere, is debased. The child poet grants that Abe is "a good old soul," even while debasing that "soul" by describing him "washing his face"—the "upward" or "cosmic aspect" of the character—in a "toilet bowl," representing the lower, earthly, "purely bodily aspect" of the poem's comic hero. Bakhtin argues that grotesque literature obeys the "peculiar logic of the 'inside out' (*à l'envers*), of the 'turnabout,' of the continual shifting from top to bottom, from front to rear, of numerous parodies and travesties, humiliations, profanations, comic crownings and uncrownings" (11). These poems also obey that logic, sending the admired Abraham Lincoln hurtling out a window with his "dick in his hand," proclaiming hyperbolically, "I'm superman," foreshadowing his imminent—and embarrassing—fall.

Bakhtin notes that carnivalesque literature concerns unfettered "images of the human body with its food, drink, defecation, and sexual life" (18). Likewise, the "your mama" poems debase the generally privileged mother, as in the second example where the mother's womb, a site of birth and sexual activity, is conflated with the anus, a site of defecation. The carnivalesque "degrades," which, to Bakhtin, means to "concern oneself with the lower stratum of the body, the life of the belly and the reproductive organs; it therefore relates to acts of defecation and copulation, conception, pregnancy, and birth" (21). If the face and head relate to the cosmic, the celestial, the spiritual, the child poet of "I fucked your mama" debases the mother by fucking her "Till she went blind," rendering useless the eyes, the windows to the soul, the organs of control and observation, which to the child may seem panoptic in scope. The poet also comments on her bad breath: the mouth, so ready with orders and admonitions (and, yes, with praise and love), is bodily. The child poet describes the head—the site of the brain and the originator of rules—as an offensive place, even as the lower stratum is celebrated: despite her bad breath and her blind eyes, her ability "to grind" more than compensates. The mother in the third example is distinguished by hyperbolic exaggeration of the lower stratum. She may be "a good old soul," but that good soul is nothing compared to her "ten-ton pussy" and her "rubber ass-hole."

These rather extreme examples are not, to be sure, the most sensitive or lyrical pieces. Altieri holds that lyricism "is a term applicable to all attempts to use what literature can exemplify as a model for affirming in ostensibly secular forms predicates about the mind, person, and society that were the basic images of dignity and value in religious or 'organic' cultures" (13). These poems are not concerned with "images of dignity." They are not designed for subtlety. In "Education by Poetry" Frost writes, "Poetry begins in trivial metaphors, petty metaphors, 'grace' metaphors, and goes on to the profoundest thinking that we have" (36). These poems are not, however, concerned with the mind, but with the body. They are composed and performed with the aim of producing strong, *bodily* reaction: laughter, guffaws, gasps, groans, or in the case of jump-rope rhymes, facilitating vigorous play. Schoolchildren sit in desks much of the day and are asked not to visit with neighbors, not to cut-up, not to laugh. Even the most natural of bodily functions requires a pass from the teacher, and children learn quickly about the taboos of flatulence. Thus, it is not surprising that the poems children perform in the playground center on taboo subjects. They problematize the mind/body split, unceasingly reminding us that we are physical, material, even as they revel in group play, exchange, and unrestrained noise. Unlike mainstream adult poetry, which is chiefly experienced in isolation, while reading in softly lit studies or in hushed recital halls or coffeehouses, the success of a playground rhyme hinges upon, as Josepha Sherman and T. K. F. Weisskopf write, "the audience's reaction" (16), which is a direct, present reaction.

The poems previously mentioned are obviously situated in the tradition of "playing the dozens," a particularly carnivalesque activity that Henry Louis Gates, Jr., discusses in *The Signifying Monkey*. Gates reminds us that the dozens, the toast, and Signifying Monkey tales have been "generally recorded from male poets, in predominately male settings such as barrooms, pool halls, and street corners." Furthermore, as is so apparent in these poems, they generally have "a phallocentric bias" (54). Thus, it might seem surprising that the playground poems we have discussed, and others like them, have been predominately composed and disseminated by young girls skipping rope, not in barrooms, but in playgrounds and on city streets. Gates notes that "Signifyin(g) itself can be, and is, undertaken with equal facility and effect by women as well as men," referring us to storyteller Gloria Hall's versions of the Signifying Monkey poems (54). The poems, with their exaggeration of male pride, power, and desire, mock the patriarchy even as they contain sexist language. (Let's recall, Lincoln is *not* Superman, and his inflated opinion of himself will, the poem suggests, earn him at the very least a nasty bump on the head.) It is curious that Gates does not discuss more extensively children's skipping rhymes, as here the tradition is quite evident, quite firmly in the hands of girls—and not exclusively girls from an African American background.

The one skipping rhyme Gates discusses is a parody, a common type of playground rhyme. First recorded by Roger D. Abrahams in *Positively Black,* the rhyme reads:

> Two, four, six, eight,
> We ain't gonna integrate.
> Eight, six, four, two,
> Bet you sons-of-bitches do. (2)

Luke Etta Hill, the East Texas teacher who collected the poem, "reported hearing some of her [third grade] students jumping to the rhyme" (Abrahams 2). All of the students were female. Abrahams maintains that through rhymes such as these "the great Civil Rights movement has become enshrined in the oral traditions of the young," arguing that "the explosiveness of the verbal exchanges between whites and blacks during that time is somehow defused by relegating these sentiments to use in play" (2). However, Abrahams appears not to recognize the poem as parody, failing to note the probable source of the children's rhyme, a source that exists outside the world of playground poetry.

Gates maintains that the rhyme was written in response to another rhyme, one that was used to resist or mock the authority of the federal government. It is important to note that the source rhyme is not a playground rhyme. Unlike the skipping rhyme recorded by Abrahams, the source is a cheer, a rallying cry—one that is not exclusively intended for children, but instead involves both child and adult participants in a public sphere. The original rhyme, first recorded in Little Rock, Arkansas, in September 1957, was chanted by both adults and children, though the rhyme was led by Anglo-American, Central High cheerleaders, who, according to Gates, "chanted in the most threatening tones":

> Two, four, six, eight,
> We don't want to integrate. (104)

Gates elaborates on the East Texas parody and its historical moment:

> This rhyme repeats and then reverses a rhyme that was chanted by white racists during the problematical integration of a Little Rock, Arkansas, high school in 1957. Although I was a child, I vividly remember hearing this chant on the news and the circumstances that occasioned its use. Each morning during the initial days of this integration attempt, white adults and their children lined either side of the school walk and hurled vicious racial epithets at the black children attempting to attend this previously all-white public school and at the members of the National Guard who had been ordered by President Eisenhower to escort and protect these children. (103–04)

Gates argues that the East Texas rhyme "signifies upon its racist antecedent," which it does marvelously, and in carnivalesque fashion.

In her excellent memoir for children, *Through My Eyes,* Ruby Bridges recalls a similar chant outside her New Orleans elementary school, another candidate for the East Texas source poem. Bridges, just starting first grade, was attempting to attend the recently desegregated William Frantz Public School in November 1960. She notes the "carnival" atmosphere in front of the school, writing, "There were barricades and people shouting and policemen everywhere. I thought maybe it was Mardi Gras, the carnival that takes place in New Orleans every year. Mardi Gras was always noisy" (16). She quotes from the November 15, 1960, issue of the *New York Times:* "Some 150 whites, mostly housewives and teenage youths, clustered along the sidewalks across from the William Frantz School when pupils marched in at 8:40 a.m. One youth chanted, 'Two, four, six, eight, we don't want to integrate; eight, six, four, two, we don't want a chigeroo'" (qtd. in Bridges 16).

Regardless of which of these cheers is the antecedent, the East Texas playground rhyme remains more interesting formally. Again, the two racist cheers are resistant, arguing against the power of the federal government to legislate integration. However, the cheers are both monologic, whereas the parody is polyvocal, heteroglossic, repeating verbatim the first stanza of its racist precursor, and confronting it directly with "bet you sons-of-bitches do." Thus the second poem is dialogic, presenting two sides of the debate, though obviously privileging the second. The second voice directly opposes the sentiment of the first; just as the third line—"Eight, six, four, two"—perfectly reverses the first series of numbers. Unlike the reversal in the New Orleans source poem ("eight, six, four, two, / we don't want a chigeroo"), the parody's reversal accentuates the message of the poem, suggesting that although the logic of the first voice may be culturally dominant, the supposedly backward thinking of the second voice may *become* dominant, this possibility enhanced by the rough music of the last line: the staccato punch of the accented bilabial [b]'s adorned by the sibilant [s]'s and affricative [č] of *bitches.* As resistant as the probable source poems are, they nonetheless represent the dominant ideology of the community in which they were chanted. In the parody, although the order of the first is deemed numerically "correct" and linear, the inverted order of the second, created in resistance to the first, remains functional in terms of the jumping game *and* the formal restrictions of the poem's rhyme scheme. Carnival allows the playful reimagining of the world, the reversal and dismantling of hierarchies; the East Texas playground rhyme formally and thematically demonstrates that these reversals can be viable.

Gates points out that the dozens (and signifying in general) has less to do with "making fun of"—parodying to ridicule—than it has to do with simply "making fun"—that is, "the play of language itself" (68). Of course, not all playground rhymes participate so directly in the tradition of the dozens as those examined thus far, though many do comment on, lampoon, and parody the adult poetic tradition, playing with and objectifying preexisting texts, "making fun" *with* (not necessarily *of*) texts provided by adult culture. In "The Rejection of Closure" Lyn Hejinian writes, "Children objectify language when they render it their plaything, in jokes, puns, and riddles, or in glossolaliac chants and rhymes" (278). It is the playground poet's tendency to "objectify language," to turn it into a "plaything," specifically in regard to parodies, that I would like to turn to now. The East Texas parody discussed earlier demonstrates the playful objectification of language so common in playground poetry. And indeed even the trio of "Good Old Soul" rhymes are parodies of a kind, recalling the famous nursery rhyme "Old King Cole Was a Merry Old Soul," extending the source poem's rather tame critique of authority to carnivalesque heights—or, rather, lows. The playfulness of playground rhymes is apparent, but what is not so apparent is the sophistication and coherence of playground parodies.

Parody is common in children's poetry. Adults writing for children have commonly used the device, Lewis Carroll most famously and, arguably, most successfully. In *Knock at a Star,* the Kennedys discuss parodic poems, calling them "take-offs." They tell their child readers, "[S]ometimes it's fun, when you're singing a song or saying a poem to make changes in it. Just for the nonsense of it, you substitute a word or two of your own for a word or two of the poet's. [Then,] you're well on your way to writing a take-off—also called a parody" (118). As an example, the Kennedys cite Kenneth Koch's well-known "Variation on a Theme by William Carlos Williams," a playful parody of Williams's "This Is Just to Say." Jack, the child protagonist of Sharon Creech's verse novel *Love That Dog* (2001), also parodies a Williams poem, "The Red Wheelbarrow," a poem that is often anthologized for children and commonly taught in the classroom. In this poem Jack writes that he doesn't "understand" Williams's poem, or why, as Williams writes, "so much depends / upon" the rain-glazed wheelbarrow and the "white / chickens." Jack's lack of comprehension, which in my experience is shared by many readers, leads him to wonder just what makes a poem a poem, asking, finally, if "any words" can make a poem, as long as the poet

> make[s]
>
> short
>
> lines. (3)

It is important to note that Jack's poem, as resistant as it is, is considerably less violent than Koch's famous parody, which approaches the level of violence so regularly found in playground poetry and its close cousin, the nursery rhyme, as the speaker wants to apologize for not only chopping "down the house that you had been saving to live in next summer," spraying the hollyhocks with lye, and giving "away the money that you had been saving to live on for the next ten years," but also for breaking his lover's leg (during an evening of dancing): "Forgive me. I was clumsy and / I wanted you here in the wards, where I am the doctor!" This final line—jokingly evoking the fact that Williams was a medical doctor—suggests a demented playfulness:

the doctor so loves his patient that he breaks his (or her) leg in order to se-
cure his lover's continuous (and helpless) presence. Likewise, Koch so loves
Williams's work that he is willing to "break" it in order to bring Williams
closer, to secure their relationship (who, after all, can read "This Is Just to
Say" the same way after encountering Koch's variations—they are forever
linked).

Jack's poem emerges from a different place, however, one not rooted in
affection, but, instead, in incomprehension and puzzlement. Thus, Creech's
narrative—and Jack's little parody—challenges a failing in poetry pedagogy,
one that Carroll similarly challenges in his *Alice* books. Students are gener-
ally not provided an officially sanctioned space to feel frustrated, angry, or
resentful toward works of official school poetry, especially, as Carroll points
out, toward the more didactic pieces. Miss Stretchberry, the instructor in
Creech's novel, provides her student with such an outlet, creating a sanc-
tioned space to parody works that are normally presented as verbal icons to
be revered. Furthermore, Miss Stretchberry crafts for Jack a space in which
he can *play* with Williams's text's formal devices and thereby voice his frus-
tration creatively, productively.

Commenting on the lack of energetic and multivalent interaction be-
tween student and poem so common in the classroom, Jed Rasula writes:

> Students are not often given affirmation that the meddlesome quality of
> a literary work should be preserved, let alone drawn out; rather, they are
> taught to "appreciate" literature, which easily translates into a directive to
> keep complaints private and squelch discomfort; or, in more authoritarian
> circumstances, given to understand that whatever they think can and may be
> used against them, and that it is better by far to recapitulate what has been
> sanctioned. (133)

Rasula concentrates on students' stifled resistant tendencies, omitting po-
tentially playful responses, whereas Creech's parody foregrounds the inter-
face between resistance and play, demonstrating a profound insight into the
poetic tradition of the playground rhyme, and perhaps even into the poetic
enterprise itself. Jack's poem can hardly be classified as carnivalesque, yet it
does foreground the parodic, resistant, and playful impulse so often found
in playground poetry, mocking Williams's piece even as it employs its domi-
nant (albeit most obvious) formal trait. Creech understands the child's im-
pulse to play with poetic tradition, whereas the Kennedys, in gently assur-
ing the child that it is okay to compose parodies, come across as somewhat
naïve. If the vast number of rhyming parodies collected by folklorists is any
indication, children hardly need to be encouraged to compose parodic po-
etry, and as we shall see, the poems produced are not always as affectionate
as Koch's parody of Williams.

The most well-known set of parodies in the canon of playground rhymes surely must be the many variations on Isaac Watts's hymn "Joy to the World." With these poems, playground poets join ranks with Lewis Carroll in using Watts's verse as a source for poetry. Like Carroll's parody "How Doth the Little Crocodile," these parodies are generally violent and involve death. The graphic violence in these parodies directly opposes Watts's own aspirations for his verse. Watts conceived his poetry as "a constant Furniture, for the Minds of Children, that they may have something to think about when alone," as an antidote to the "shocking and bloody histories, [and] wanton songs or amorous romances" they might encounter (qtd. in Styles 14). Though "Joy to the World" was not originally intended for a child audience, since its adoption as a common Christmas carol it has become associated with children and the increasingly child-centered holiday, which probably explains why child poets have adopted the hymn as a convenient scaffolding for their purposes.

Based on Psalm 96:11–13, the hymn's religious theme is in conflict with its schoolyard variations. The second verse of Watts's hymn reads:

> Joy to the world, the Savior reigns!
> Let men their songs employ;
> While fields and floods, rocks, hills and plains
> Repeat the sounding joy,
> Repeat the sounding joy,
> Repeat, repeat, the sounding joy.

Whereas "Joy to the World" describes the "fields and floods, rocks, hills and plains" resounding with joy at their Lord's arrival from above, the playground versions question the hierarchical values implied by the hymn. For example, one version reads:

> Joy to the world, the school burned down,
> And all the teachers died.
> We're going to take the principal
> And hang her from the toilet bowl
> With a rope around her neck,
> A rope around her neck,
> A rope, a rope around her neck. (Sherman and Weisskopf 113)

In Watts's version the world "receive[s] her King" gladly, the "nations prove / the glories of His righteousness." Not so in the playground version, which inverts the normal power relationships between teacher and student, principal and class clown. Authority—whether king or principal—is not revered in the playground, and, using conventional carnivalesque imagery, the head—the site of the intellect—is noosed and hung surrealistically "from the toilet bowl." Of course, the parody's primary target is not Watts's verse, but school culture itself. Again, the child poet is making fun *with* Watts's hymn, not necessarily *of* it.

In another variation the poet chants, "Joy to the world, my teacher's dead, / I chopped right off his head." The head and all it symbolizes is cut from the teacher, and in mock sensitivity the child poet assures us that we need not "worry 'bout the body [because] / I flushed it down the potty" (113). Sherman and Weisskopf note that this "caricatured, almost ritualized violence" is an embodiment of the child poets' "resentment over having their days structured and their freedom curtailed" by school officials and parents (103). Instead of "engaging in actual violence," most children release their frustrations through poems such as these, poems that employ consistent imagery and balanced form; as exemplified, for instance, in this two-stanza version, collected from an eleven-year-old girl and a nine-year-old boy:

> Joy to the world, the teacher's dead,
> We barbecued her head.
> What happened to her body?
> We flushed it down the potty.
> And around and around it went,
> And around and around it went,
> And around and around and around it went.
>
> Joy to the world, the school burned down,
> And all the teachers are dead.
> If you're looking for the principal,
> He's hanging from the flagpole
> With a rope around his neck,
> With a rope around his neck,
> With a rope, a rope around his neck. (Sherman and Weisskopf
>   113)

Certainly this piece is not designed for adult ears, especially in these post-Columbine times. Its hyperbolic violence, however, might distract most listeners from its sophisticated structure. The poem uses parallelism to interesting effect. Both stanzas refer to fire: in stanza 1 the teacher's head is barbecued; in stanza 2 the school is torched. Just as the teacher's head is a metonym for the mind and the authority that insists children sit still and develop theirs, so too is the school that houses that authority. Both are subjected to fire, both destroyed by flame in a strangely bacchanalian sacrifice. More parallelism occurs in the third line of both stanzas. There the poet directly addresses the reader (or auditor), implicating us in the acts of rebellion, as if we are asking where the young rebels hid the teacher's body, as if we are looking for the principal, perhaps to do him in ourselves. But the most compelling symmetry concerns upward and downward movement, recalling the inverted cosmology of carnival. In the first stanza the teacher's body is flushed *down* the toilet, transformed into waste, while in the second the principal is strung *up,* taking place of the flag, the symbol of freedom, to which children are often encouraged to pledge their allegiance each morning. The school is burned down, converted to ash, while the principal, the ultimate (male) authority of school, is hoisted up, the Earth's downward pull putting an end to the students' "curtailed" freedom. The principal becomes a perverse flag of child-rule, maintaining his elevated status only as a corpse, devoid of intellect or spirit.

The "Joy to the World" parodies also demonstrate how playground poems are embodied through oral performance. Unlike official school poetry, which is frequently described using musical terminology and metaphors, playground poetry commonly incorporates music and melody. These poems are rooted in the oral tradition of the nursery rhyme—the tradition of Mother Goose. They are not poems for the page. Rather, playground rhymes are often lyrical in the original sense of the word: musical, sung to the lyre. However, whether the poems are chanted or sung, they invariably involve body movement. Just as the bodies described in the poems are often contorted and exaggerated in hyperbolic fashion, the bodies of the performers are moving in time with the chant, dancing along with the melody. Playground poetry is embodied through melody, intricate clapping games, hand gestures, and elaborate jump-rope techniques. Again, the body has preeminence in these poems. Furthermore, sometimes the body movements are necessary to understand the literal meaning of the rhyme. Consider this poem a student of mine remembers chanting in Chicago:

> Mama's in the kitchen burning that rice,
> Daddy's on the corner shooting that dice,
> Brother's in jail raising that hell
> Sister's on the corner selling fruit cocktail.

She reports that the rhyme is chanted, not sung, and the last three syllables are heavily accented, involving corresponding hand gestures that illuminate the last line's double entendre. Upon each word, the performer grips first the breasts, then the groin, then the buttocks: "fruit, cock, tail."

The last poem I will discuss is perhaps one of the best-known playground rhymes, the infamous "Ms. Lucy" hand-clapping rhyme, which serves as an exemplar of the playfulness of playground poetry and as a convenient transition to chapter 4, which deals with rhymes existing in the borderlands between playground and official school poetry. Although domesticated playground poems most definitely employ elements of the carnivalesque discussed above, they do so only to a limit, and this limit is one set by the social codes of the culture in which they were produced:

> Ms. Lucy had a steamboat, the steamboat had a bell.
> Ms. Lucy went to heaven and the steamboat went to . . .
> *Hello* operator, please give me number nine,
> And if you disconnect me I will chop off your . . .
> *Behind* the refrigerator, there was a piece of glass.
> Ms. Lucy sat upon it and it went right up her . . .
> *Ask* me no more questions, I'll tell you no more lies.
> The boys are in the bathroom pulling down their . . .
> *Flies* are in the meadow, the meadow's in the park.
> The boys and girls are kissing in the
> D.A.R.K. D.A.R.K. D.A.R.K. dark dark dark.
> The dark is like a movie, a movie's like a show
> A show is like the TV set, and that is all I know . . .
> I know I know my mother, I know I know my pop
> I know I know my sister with the 18-hour
> 18-hour 18-hour bra bra bra. (Sherman and Weisskopf 33–34)[5]

"Ms. Lucy" foregrounds embodiment not only through the elaborate hand clapping that often accompanies performance, but also in its morphological play, which works as well on the page as off. This poem plays with language at the level of sentence and word simultaneously. It violates sentence boundaries, disrupting conventional narrative flow, even as it blurs the lines between one word and the next, calling attention to the materiality of word, the plasticity of language, using that plasticity to navigate the border between social acceptability and taboo.

The poem is perplexing imagistically, almost surreal. Guided by shared morphological and phonological elements, it drifts from one setting to the next, one image cluster to another. But there is a strange sense that can be made of the poem. The images vacillate between two topics, sex and punishment, sometimes suggesting that sex *is* punishment. Formally, the poem foregrounds its awareness of and begrudging respect for appropriateness and decorum. It takes its interest in sexuality and violence only so far and then pulls back, testing the flexibility of rules instead of flagrantly breaking them. The adult listener (or perhaps the snitch) is implied in the form. As Sherman and Weisskopf write, the poem has a certain "attraction for children: when caught by adults, those children can say in feigned innocence, 'We were just singing a song . . .'" (206).[6] In fact, the poem itself seems a symptom of the desire to transgress without transgressing.

Though it is the steamboat and not Ms. Lucy that goes to hell, the poem seems preoccupied with those issues that, conventionally, might land one there. The first two lines, with their almost arbitrary judgments on Lucy and the steamboat, suggest the seemingly arbitrary verdicts doled out by adult authority figures. Yet within the logic of the poem it is appropriate that the steamboat go to hell, with its phallic smokestacks, its bell and clapper implying a sexuality that will be made overtly Oedipal by the poem's end. Even the operator, responsible for correct connections, is vaguely sexual. I cannot help but recall Carl Sandburg's poem "Manual System," in which he describes Mary, a telephone operator who "has a thingamajig clamped on her ears / And sits all day taking plugs out and sticking plugs in" (1–2).

A tension in the poem exists between the desire to articulate sexual curiosity and a desire to censor that curiosity. The punishments themselves, which are never really realized, thanks to morphological transformation, highlight the ambivalence. On the one hand, the poet sends the steamboat to hell, perhaps for being too steamy, and on the other, the poet threatens to punish the operator if she "disconnect[s]" the speaker from whomever he or she is speaking to (perhaps a girlfriend or boyfriend?). The first might elicit (or at least symbolize) sexual desire, while the other holds the potential to disconnect it. Both are punished. The poem then moves from the painful image of Lucy sitting on a shard of glass (described in unabashedly sexual terms: "it went right up her . . .") to a voyeuristic look at boys "in the bathroom pulling down their . . ." Here we have the most overtly sexual moment in the poem, one tied to the carnivalesque by its conflation of erotic desire with waste, the voyeuristic impulse to watch others urinate.

We might argue that many children do not, as they clap along to "Ms. Lucy," consider the thematic interrelationship of the various images, but certainly they understand their consistent tone, that they all belong in the same poem. As Francelia Butler reminds us:

> Some adults are surprised, even shocked, to learn that many children's rhymes, including those for skipping, have an unmistakably sexual, sometimes even

bawdy, element. In some, the bawdy aspect is too broad to appeal to refined tastes. I have heard children skipping [to] such rhymes, totally unselfconsciously. Whether they understood in all cases the meaning of the rhymes is hard to tell. What is certain is that children, as they grow up, become secretly fascinated with erotic content. After all, what child has not wondered about what goes on between parents behind the closed doors of their bedroom. (53)

"Ms. Lucy" builds to this very thought, the mysteries within the parents' bedroom. We move from "boys and girls [. . .] kissing in the dark" to a curious chain of similes: "The dark is like a movie, a movie's like a show / A show is like a TV set, and that is all I know." But despite claims to the contrary, it seems that this is not all the speaker knows, for in line 14 we return again to a male and female pairing, the speaker's "mother" and "pop." This pairing and its placement in the poem suggest another kind of show a child might encounter in the dark, the Freudian Primal Scene. Thus, the voyeuristic impulse in lines 8 and 10, the scopophilic desire to see "The boys [. . .] in the bathroom" and "The boys and girls [. . .] kissing" is linked with the desire to know "what goes on between parents behind the closed doors of their bedroom."

In *Interpretation of Dreams* Freud calls this desire "uncanny," as it "arouses anxiety within [the child]" (624). With its neatly subverted violent impulses, surrealistic dreamlike imagery and shifts, and its preoccupation with kissing in the dark and evocation of the mother and the father, this poem certainly fits Freud's description of the child's response to the primal scene: "a sexual excitation with which their understanding is unable to cope and which they also [. . .] repudiate because their parents are involved" (624). Laura Mulvey reminds us that Freud's discussion of scopophilia in his *Three Essays on Sexuality* revolves "around the voyeuristic activities of children, their desire to see and make sure of the private and the forbidden (curiosity about another people's genital and bodily functions, about the presence and absence of the penis and, retrospectively, about the primal scene)" (16). Indeed, if Mulvey is correct in noting that scopophilic pleasure hinges on the objectification of whoever is being watched, then the poem's preoccupation with the objectification of language itself resonates perfectly with the poem's theme, even down to the last image of the sister in her "18-hour bra." She is being spied upon.

The emphasis on "the dark" in lines 11 and 12 recalls Mulvey's argument that the voyeuristic pleasure of cinema (the "movie" in line 12) hinges on "the extreme contrast between the darkness in the auditorium (which also isolates the spectators from one another) and the brilliance of the shifting patterns of light and shade on the screen," a contrast that ultimately "helps to promote the illusion of voyeuristic separation" (17). This darkness, this "voyeuristic separation," along with the formal pulling away from inappropriate language and issues, tempers the potentially traumatic experience of the primal scene. The violence, the "chop[ping]" and damnation, suggests an understanding of the violation involved in such spying, and perhaps a reckoning of the "primal" nature of sex, its potentially violent dimension. As Freud writes in his *Three Essays,* "If children [. . .] witness sexual intercourse between adults [. . .] they inevitably regard the sexual act as a sort of ill-treatment or act of subjugation: they view it, that is, in a sadistic sense" (62). This view helps explain the violent undercurrents in "Ms. Lucy." Furthermore, Freud's insight that children "usually seek a solution of the mystery [of their sadistic interpretation of sex] in some common activity concerned with the function of micturition or defaecation" provides a suitable explanation for mother and pop's link to the bathroom humor of "The boys are in the bathroom" (62).

The poem's attraction to children lies in its working through competing impulses, the desire to see, the desire to know, and the urge to repress those desires, to submerge them, just as the steamboat is submerged. In this respect the poem is unusual for a playground rhyme, as it is uninterested in unrestrained play, in carnivalesque reversal of hierarchy, the unabashed celebration of the body. It is cleaned up, sanitized. Whether it is sanitized for the child's benefit, or, more subversively, in order to test boundaries in the presence of adults, depends, I suppose, on the child who is performing the rhyme. Either way, this rhyme moves toward the classroom; it operates in two realms at once and can be performed near authority without much fear of punishment, whereas the other playground rhymes are meant exclusively for young ears.

As seen in the "Joy to the World" parodies, the spirit of playground poetry resists and playfully engages repressive elements of adult culture through the linguistic play of carnival. It inspires children to construct their own tradition, to compose their own poetry, to teach themselves. "Ms. Lucy" is more like the poems discussed in the next chapter—the somewhat subversive poems of John Ciardi and Shel Silverstein and the nonsense of Theodore Roethke—than other playground rhymes. The carnivalesque impulse of the poem operates within the framework of wider (adult) cultural norms of decorum and punishment/retribution for the violation of these norms.

Often as children grow older they neither maintain a taste for playground poetry nor develop a taste for official school poetry. Because teachers and other adults fail to tap into the playful spirit of playground poetry, there is no mechanism for bridging the distance between what appears to be outdoor freedom of expression and indoor repression.

Unlike adult verse, playground poetry is owned and reinvented by each new generation of children, and therein lies its power. Testifying to the fact that poetry is a heterogeneous discourse that operates in multiple registers and serves multiple purposes, playground poetry is worthy of consideration alongside the adult poetic traditions that are usually privileged in the classroom. Yet perhaps bringing playground poetry into the classroom would somehow diminish it, take away its charm and power. Or perhaps bringing it into the classroom, the living room, perhaps treating playground poetry *as* poetry, talking about it with children, singing it alongside them, perhaps such a dialogue could lead both children and adults to an enriched understanding of poetry and the communities that produce it.

It's worth the risk.

4

Street Cries
Mother Goose, Urchin Poetry, and Contemporary U.S. Children's Poetry

God bless the roots!—Body and soul are one
The small become the great, the great the small;
The right thing happens to the happy man.

Theodore Roethke, "The Right Thing"

In "David McCord's Poems: Something Behind the Door," Myra Cohn Livingston praises McCord's children's poetry, contrasting his work with that written by "poets who would ask us to listen to their precious inner psyches, their confessions, dreams and lies, their poverty-stricken self-directed wishes," poetry she associates with the "raw" side of the anthology wars (157). Her essay calls for a return to a mid-century poetic, one that is implicitly academic and professionalized, exemplified by the tightly crafted nature poems and genial light verse of David McCord, whom she champions. She decries the turn to the "garbage delight" of poets like Dennis Lee, lamenting "the inadequacies of form and truth and glorification of the unconscious" that have been, in her words, "invading children's poetry [. . .] and assault[ing] literature itself" (158).[1] This chapter seeks to complicate traditional understandings of so-called garbage delight—a problematic, if quite popular, strain of children's poetry—even as it reimagines its historical and stylistic roots. Demonstrating this mode of poetry's connections to and departures from both playground poetry and nursery rhyme, this chapter points to Theodore Roethke and John Ciardi (two poets whom Livingston often cites approvingly) as foundational practitioners of "garbage delight," exploring their relationship to each other and to the later practitioners Jack Prelutsky and Shel Silverstein.[2] Finally, it conceptualizes these poems not as "garbage," but rather as *domesticated* playground poetry produced and disseminated by adults with complicated and often differing interests.

Much has been written about the "inadequacies of form and truth" Livingston denounces, and many critics have come to the defense of the poetry she attacks. In *Pleasures of Children's Literature* (1996), for instance, Perry Nodelman directly refutes Livingston's position, arguing that the poets she evokes—poets "like Jack Prelutsky, Dennis Lee, Roald Dahl, and many others"—exemplify the spirit of "anarchy," providing children with an occasion "to test rules and to imagine defiance of them" (209–10). John Rowe Townsend labels these poets of "garbage delight" the school of "urchin verse" (300).[3] Though one could argue that the street cries of Mother Goose are the true roots of urchin poetry, Townsend places its beginnings in the 1970s, maintaining that British poet Michael Rosen's *Mind Your Own Business* (1974) "was the exemplar" (300). According to Townsend, urchin poetry abandons "social or literary pretension" and depicts "family life in the raw, with its backchat, fury and muddle" (300). Charting the move from the country to the city, urchin poetry is more likely to feature "disused railway lines, building sites and junkheaps" than "woods and meadows" (300).

Morag Styles similarly places the birth of urchin poetry in 1974, claiming that Rosen's book was "The first publication in this genre" (262). According to Styles, *Mind Your Own Business* "blasted onto the decorous world of children's publishing, taking many by surprise with its sheer cheek, its down-to-earth, yet comical tone, its flouting of conventions, as well as the original way in which it tapped into contemporary childhood" (263). This characterization recalls that of the playground poetry discussed in chapter 3, particularly in its reference to urchin poetry's "down-to-earth, yet comical tone." Like playground poetry, urchin poetry largely resists subtle lyricism, "flouts convention," and playfully reverses (or at least problematizes) conventional hierarchies. However, urchin poetry is older than Townsend and Styles maintain, and, curiously, this early urchin poetry is (perhaps counterintuitively) associated with the cooked side of the anthology wars rather than the raw. X. J. Kennedy, whose poetry was featured in Donald Hall and Robert Pack's *New Poets of England and America: Second Selection* (1962), looks to his own forebears for the genesis of urchin poetry, attributing the shift away from mid-century light verse and nature poetry to the technically accomplished John Ciardi, with whom he became acquainted at the Bread Loaf Writers' Conference. Specifically, Kennedy points to *The Reason for the Pelican* (1959), Ciardi's first collection of children's poetry, as the start of what we might call adult-produced playground poetry, a text released some fifteen years before Rosen's *Mind Your Own Business*.

Kennedy argues that with *Pelican* Ciardi "threw open the musty old parlor of American children's poetry, with its smell of rose petals and camphor, and he let in a blast of fresh air" (*Reason* 63). If Hall, Simpson, and Pack's rather cooked first and second selections of *New Poets of England and*

America (1957, 1962) are barometers of mainstream adult poetry of the time, the nature poem, with or without the rose petals, was common in the world of adult as well as children's poetry. In 1959, remarking on the rise of the Beat generation, Robert Langbaum was already commenting on the bankruptcy of the nature lyric so popular in the '50s, obliquely referencing Robert Frost, who, as we saw in chapter 1, had come to exemplify official school poetry: "[Our nature philosophy] connects not only man's body but his mind and culture to the primeval ooze; and you cannot convey that sense of nature in poems about the cultivated countryside of England or New England" (331). Kenneth Koch lampoons this tendency toward the "cultivated" nature lyric in his poem "Fresh Air," anthologized in Donald Allen's *New American Poetry* (1960):

> I am afraid you have never smiled at the hibernation
> Of bear cubs except that you saw in it some deep relation
> To human suffering and wishes, oh what a bunch of crackpots!
>   (7–9)

Even as Roethke plumbed the depths of "ooze," Ciardi's children's poetry veered away from the New England pastoral and came to rest squarely in the suburbs. In books like *The Monster Den* (1963), for instance, Ciardi caricatures the genteel, nineteenth-century diction that was common in mid-century children's poetry, achieving a tone similar to that of Edward Gorey's (Gorey was his student at Harvard), prefiguring Daniel Handler's *Lemony Snicket* books. As Ciardi writes in his introduction to *Mid-Century American Poets* (1950), "the nineteenth century was a great literary achievement, but it began with one dreadful flaw: it tended to take itself much too seriously" (xviii). Coupled with Gorey's distinctive illustrations, much of Ciardi's children's poetry pokes fun at that seriousness.

Ciardi's poetry does not yoke the child to nature, nor does it idealize or fetishize the child. Though *Pelican* is obviously indebted to Edward Lear, Ciardi's other books rest more comfortably in the tradition of Heinrich Hoffman's *Struwwelpeter* (1845), as they are often macabre bouts of teasing that do not shrink from inflicting harm on their youthful subjects. For instance, in "Sit Up When You Sit Down," included in Ciardi's *You Know Who* (1964), the narrator threatens to beat a naughty child with "a stick":

> And did I beat him? Goodness no!
> He took one look and he seemed to know
> Just how to sit up when he sits down.
> And now he's the very best boy in town. (14–18)

Another poem, "About the Teeth of Sharks," collected in *You Read to Me, I'll Read to You* (1962), concerns a narrator whose curiosity leads the obliging second person "you" of the poem into decapitation by a shark:

> Still closer—here, I'll hold your hat:
> Has it a third row [of teeth] behind that?
>
> Now look in and . . . Look out! Oh my,
> I'll *never* know now! Well, goodbye. (5–8)

Hearkening back to the punning jests of A. A. Milne and Lewis Carroll, these poems illustrate the level of language play that is so common in Ciardi's children's poetry. Both make a clever turn on prepositional double meaning and incongruity (looking out and looking in, sitting up and sitting down) even as they highlight Ciardi's willingness to turn the tables on the child, to use the caricatured violence of playground poetry in the service of good-natured teasing.

Between 1959 and 1966 Ciardi published nine books for children, among them *The Man Who Sang the Sillies* (1961), winner of the Boys' Clubs of America Junior Book Award, and *The King Who Saved Himself from Being Saved* (1965), a self-referential fairy tale in verse. In addition to authoring these children's books, Ciardi was also a very popular lecturer, supplementing his income and his fame by penning a regular column for the *Saturday Review* (boosting sales with his provocative positions) and hosting "a weekly cultural magazine show" for CBS Television called *Accent* (Cifelli 263). These various projects, coupled with his association with the prestigious Bread Loaf Writers' Conference, kept Ciardi in the public eye and ensured his role as an uncommonly famous public intellectual. Edward M. Cifelli notes that some of Ciardi's success—and his boastfulness—alienated him "from the generation of younger poets, who [. . .] had not known him in his years of struggle" (241), boastfulness that found its way even into his children's poetry. Ciardi jokes about his celebrity status and the money such status affords in "While I Was Shaving" (1966), in which his son asks:

> [. . .] When I'm as old as you,
> Will I be fat and funny, too?
> And will I be rich? That Billy Fitch
> Says his father says you're rich.
> I *hope* it's true. If it *is* true,
> Someday will I be rich as you? (28–33)

Though Ciardi jests, his cultural weight was no joke, and thus his entrance into the world of children's literature helped modify how the poetic establishment viewed children's poetry, even as his poems offered a prototype for urchin poetry to come. X. J. Kennedy argues that Ciardi was "responsible to a large extent for [the] change in climate" that allowed "a poet to publish a collection of children's verse without being exiled from the literary republic" (*Reason* 61). Undoubtedly Kennedy is correct. Ciardi bestowed his aura to the writing of children's poetry.

Not two years after the publication of *Reason for the Pelican,* Theodore Roethke, another poet who utilized the tropes of playground poetry in his work for children, joined Ciardi, publishing *I Am! Says the Lamb* (1961) with Doubleday. This collection features poetry Roethke had been working on for quite a number of years and certainly, as Livingston writes, "glorif[ies] [. . .] the unconscious" ("David McCord's Poems" 158). "The Lost Son," one of Roethke's most celebrated works, is a psychological drama brimming with symbols from the unconscious and, as such, is not too terribly unlike much of his children's poetry. In "Open Letter," a preface written especially for his selections in *Mid-Century American Poets,* Roethke notes that "The Lost Son" "telescope[s] image and symbol[, . . .] speak[ing] in a kind of psychic shorthand" (71). Roethke explains that this "psychic shorthand" emerges through the use of "technical effects" with quite auspicious ancestors, among them "German and English folk literature, particularly Mother Goose," playground poetry's selfsame ancestors (70). It is "the spring and rush of the child" Roethke seeks, and he achieves it through the use of short line, accentual meter, and "compelling and immediate" language (71). As he writes in his notebook: "The decasyllable line is fine for someone who wants to meditate—or maunder. Me, I need something to jump in: hence the spins and shifts, the songs, the rants and howls. The shorter line can still serve us: it did when English was young, and when we were children" ("Words" 93). In addition to the short line, Roethke, more than Ciardi, freely borrows from nursery rhymes' reservoir of symbols. In "Some Remarks on Rhythm," a fascinating account of the "technical effects" mentioned above, Roethke claims: "[P]oetry is shot through with appeals to the unconsciousness, to the fears and desires that go far back into our childhood, into the imagination of the race." He continues, remarking, "[S]ome words, like *hill, plow, mother, window, bird, fish,* are so drenched with human associations, they sometimes can make even bad poems evocative" (71). Roethke's children's poetry, both his nonsense and greenhouse poems, uniformly concern nature and the world, rhythms, and symbols of the nursery rhyme; and thus the natural world that emerges from his children's poetry is manifestly different from that of, say, McCord's. Roethke's nonsense, with its taunting wit and "cheek," participates in the urchin paradigm, though of course it abstains from the urban images that are common in both Ciardi's work and later urchin poetry.

Consider, for instance, Roethke's "The Lady and the Bear," which features a "Pee-culiar" bear who fishes with his paw (as, we are told, "Biddly Bears" are wont to do). The titular lady is amazed at this technique, so much so that she:

> [. . .] slipped from the Bank
> And fell in the Stream still clutching a Plank,
> But the Bear just sat there until she Sank;
> As he went on fishing his way, his way,
> As he went on fishing his way. (26–30)

No doubt there is a moral involved here, and perhaps one of autobiographical significance, as the rather hulking poet considered himself "as a sort of dancing bear" (Hamilton 335). In "Four for Sir John Davies," Hamilton reminds us, Roethke writes, "And I have made a promise to my ears / I'll sing and whistle dancing bears" (5–6). Quite the careerist, Roethke no doubt would appreciate his bear's dedication to his personal method, his drive to keep "on fishing his way" despite gawkers. The poem may also speak to Roethke's dedication to writing darkly comic, unconventional children's poetry. The dark comedy of the poem emerges from the apathy the bear feels for the unfortunate woman. The poem ends with him fishing and the woman drowning, an uncommon finish for a children's poem. Robert Leydenfrost's apt illustration depicts a bear happily gazing at the reader, two high-heeled legs poking upward from the water.

Other poems in *I Am!* are similar to what Sherman and Weisskopf call the "gross-out" tradition of playground poetry, poems that "exist as a means of letting off steam, rebelling against the societal strictures, food rules, and safety restrictions set by adults" (16). One of these pieces, called "Goo Girl," revels in the disgusting eating habits and cat-frightening flatulence of an unnamed turtle, to whom the poem is addressed:

> The *Things* you do, Nobody does:
> Putting Egg in your Shoe
> And then making Goo,
> Which, with Slobbers and Snorts,
> You drink up in Quarts;
> And that Gravy and Fat
> All over your hat—

How *Did* you do *That*?

When you Slurp and go, Poof!

The Cat runs for a Roof

Clear under the Chair;

And your friends—how they Stare! (2–13)

Roethke's choice of imagery (particularly that of lines 3 to 6) is fitting, re-calling playground poems like "Gopher Guts," which similarly deals with the consumption of seemingly inedible materials. Consider, for example, this version of "Gopher Guts," collected by Sherman and Weisskopf, which dates from the 1960s:

Great green gobs of greasy, grimy gopher guts,

Mutilated monkey meat,

Little birdies' dirty feet.

Great green gobs of greasy, grimy gopher guts,

And I forgot my spoon. (17)

To some people "Goo-Girl"—like "Gopher Guts"—may appear tasteless. Nevertheless, it stays true to Roethke's larger poetic project, one that is not too different from that suggested by a vast number of playground rhymes—namely, both the inversion of traditional hierarchies and the examination of the lower stratum. Whether he is attributing sainthood to "the lopped limbs" of cuttings ("What saint strained so much?"), or scrutinizing the "Leaf-mold, manure, lime" of the root cellar, Roethke's preoccupation with the "under-ground," with the lower, with "stink" is evident throughout his poetry and throughout *I Am!* ("Cuttings: Later" 3–5; "Root Cellar" 6, 9). Randall Jarrell comments on Roethke's "love affairs" with the wet world of slime and ooze in "Fifty Years of American Poetry": "Many poets are sometimes childish; Roethke, uniquely, is sometimes babyish, though he is a powerful Donatello baby who has love affairs, and whose marsh-like unconscious is continually celebrating its marriage with the whole wet dark underside of things" (326). In short, Jarrell is noting the carnivalesque tendencies of Roethke's work. Roethke's friend (and rival) Robert Lowell also recognized these impulses: two days after Roethke's death (August 1, 1963), Lowell wrote a letter con-soling Beatrice, Roethke's wife, in which he praises the "Rabelaisian energy" permeating her husband's poetry (*Letters* 429). Although Myrtle the turtle censures the titular "Goo-Girl," the poem's charm lies in the Rabelaisian delight with which Roethke describes her hyperbolic breaches of etiquette, the comic "Slobbers and Snorts" that transform the anthropomorphized turtle into a pig. The turtle in this poem is not a creature of the "cultivated countryside of England or New England" that Robert Langbaum worries so occupied mid-century poetry. Myrtle's cousin is more akin to the "primeval ooze" and is perhaps more likely to eat it (331).

Both Ciardi and Roethke began writing children's poems in the early '50s, at the height of genteel, academic verse. Roethke's *The Waking: Poems, 1933–53* contains several selections that would appear in *I Am! Says the Lamb,* as does *Words for the Wind* (1958), which contains an "interlude" titled "Lighter Pieces and Poems for Children." In a 1953 letter to J. F. Powers, Roethke mentions a New York reading he performed "with a five piece band behind me in which, so help me, I 'sang' several songs,—settings of 'children's' poems" (*Letters* 189). This connection to music, to orality, is common in urchin poetry, just as it is common in playground verse. Roethke's arch quotations highlight his distrust of easy categories and suggest his discomfort with the current state of poetry for children (and thus his hesitance in having his work grouped within it). In a 1957 piece written for the *Poetry Book Society Bulletin* (London), Roethke comments on the children's rhymes featured in *Words for the Wind* and, by extension, his reading of the trends in mid-century children's poetry:[4] "Then by way of contrast [to the love poems early in the collection], there is a handful of light pieces and poems for children. These are rougher than what most children's editors prefer. The attempt—part of a larger effort—was to make poems which please both child and parent, without insulting the intelligence or taste of either" ("Theodore Roethke Writes" 32). No doubt this larger project involved the production of works that were specifically aimed at children, realized in *I Am! Says the Lamb* and *Party at the Zoo* (1963), his only works written expressly for children. As the examples above suggest, the poems in both of these collections are "rougher" than much of the mid-century children's poetry that predates them. However, regardless of the "rough" quality of these poems, Roethke's aim to avoid "insulting the intelligence or taste of either" adult or child is central to domesticated playground poetry, as this type of poetry addresses, by its very nature, a dual audience. In other words, domesticated poetry is a subtle form of what U. C. Knoepflmacher and Mitzi Myers call "cross-writing."[5] Though it borrows from the tropes of playground poetry discussed in chapter 3, it is somewhat sanitized, so that it will not offend adult sensibilities, even as it participates in the carnivalesque.

Though *Reason for the Pelican* was not published until 1959, a 1951 letter from Ciardi to Roethke shows that Ciardi had a completed manuscript of *Pelican* eight years before its publication: "I've got a book of children's poems due late next year. Now being illustrated. To be called THE REASON FOR THE PELICAN" (qtd. in Cifelli 253). Ciardi began writing children's poetry when first his nephews and then his own children began reading. In fact, it was his daughter Myra's difficulty learning to read that inspired him to write *I Met a Man,* an easy reader based on a first-grade reading vocabulary. Similarly, *You Read to Me, I'll Read to You* mixes basic with more advanced vocabularies. No doubt the wild success of Dr. Seuss's subversive *The Cat in the Hat* (1957) and the resultant creation of the Random House Beginner Books subsidiary produced the industry atmosphere in which Ciardi's books thrived.[6] Ciardi's books for young readers, though more violent, are imbued with Theodore Geisel's fondness for wordplay and are conceived in the same spirit: the desire for complicated, interesting poetry for beginning readers and an antidote to the banal, simplistic primers that were so common at the time. Likewise, Roethke's *Party at the Zoo* was published as a part of the Modern Masters Books for Children series, which, according to the back cover, was "a unique new series for the beginning reader by such world-famous authors as Arthur Miller, Shirley Jackson, and Robert Graves." Besides being a surrealistic nursery rhyme (the back cover brags—and rightfully so—that the collection is "an irrepressible blend of Mother Goose, Lewis Carroll, and Edward Lear"), *Party at the Zoo,* like *The Cat in the Hat,* is also a useful tool for reading acquisition, containing only 268 readily recognizable words. This desire to craft complicated, phonologically interesting poetry with an accessible vocabulary links Ciardi and Roethke, as does their great respect for younger readers.

The two poets are also linked by their preoccupation with childhood. Furthermore, they both champion Mother Goose, that magical figure who hovers perpetually over playground poetry. This familiarity with Mother Goose no doubt informs their mutual understanding of the violence so common in nursery rhymes, their insight into the teasing nature of folk poetry, playground rhymes in particular. This shared interest can be seen as early as 1950, when Ciardi published his important *Mid-Century American Poets,* an anthology that helped reify the reputations of several up-and-coming poets, including Roethke. In the introduction Ciardi writes that "the poets presented in this book are all part of what will be recognized as a poetic 'generation'" (xxvi), underlining his desire to craft a mini-canon of mid-century poets, a canon including poets like Richard Wilbur, Jarrell, and Roethke—all three of whom would publish children's poetry shortly after the release of Ciardi's first book for children. *Mid-Century* was not as successful as Ciardi would have liked. In 1953 he wrote to Roethke that "*Mid-Century Poets* has more or less petered-out and I don't know what the exact figures are, but they're not nearly what I had hoped for" (*Letters* 84). Nevertheless, despite Ciardi's pessimistic outlook, Cifelli notes the "landmark" status of the collection, citing X. J. Kennedy's 1986 claim that it "remains one of the most revealing anthologies of poetry criticism ever assembled" (qtd. in Cifelli 143). Furthermore, as Edward Brunner argues, *Mid-Century*

American Poets was effectively the "first anthology to propound a concise aesthetic for postwar poetry" (42).

In his discussion of this aesthetic, Ciardi turns to children's poetry, particularly Mother Goose, quoting "Hickory Dickory Dock" in the introduction, using it as an example of "a really difficult piece of symbolism" (xiv). Ciardi emphasizes that the delight one takes from "Hickory Dickory" has less to do with meaning per se than with "the child's pleasure of tasting the syllables on the tongue" (xv). In the introduction to his own selections in *Mid-Century*, Ciardi holds that "*poetry should be read aloud*" (249, italics in original), leaving no place for visual poetry. Yet by foregrounding the value of the sound of Mother Goose, Ciardi seems to imply that "Hickory Dickory" is a sort of sound sculpture. He argues, "[Hickory Dickory] means only what every child knows—delight. And delight is not a function of the rational mind. [. . .] To see what it does mean, you need only go and read Mother Goose to a child: you will then be observing a natural audience busy with the process of receiving poetry as it was intended to be received" (xvii). In Ciardi's view, this poem, and the others in his anthology, stands as "the final dignity of [. . .] irrationality" (xiv). Ciardi defends "Hickory Dickory" not only with appeals to its "particular combination of sounds and actions (symbolic actions?)" but also to its longevity, asking "what is there [. . .] that makes this jingle survive a long word-of-mouth transmission in the English voice-box?" (xv). Ciardi has a romantic conception of the child (and a rather monolithic one: all children, he suggests, will like Mother Goose; all children know delight). He urges his adult readers to become "like a child" when they encounter poetry, to "come prepared for delight" (xv). He asks, "If a child can do it[,] why can't you?" (xv). Arguing against what he characterizes as the willfully obscurist tendencies of high modernism, Ciardi champions the immediate accessibility that mid-century poetry offers, an immediacy he equates with nursery rhymes.

However, though Ciardi argues for the poetic value of "Hickory Dickory," he seems interested in using it primarily as a rhetorical vehicle to further his arguments concerning the proper way to read and respond to mid-century poetry for adults. Unlike Roethke, who spends considerable time and intellectual energy articulating a theory of prosody that explains the rhythmic complexity of Mother Goose (most notably in "Some Remarks on Rhythm"), Ciardi does not linger to theorize the value of "Hickory Dickory" other than to note that he enjoys it, universalizing that enjoyment to all children. Ciardi uses playground poetry in a similar manner, labeling the only playground poem he discusses as an example of the "Bad poetry [. . .] we all have in common" (xv). Ciardi divides "bad poetry" into three categories: invective, obscenity, and love-yelps (xv), the first two major categories of playground poetry. Only alluding to (but not quoting) "obscenity" (one thinks of the "your mama" poems discussed in chapter 3), he does present us with an example of invective:

> Billy, Billy, dirty coat
> Stinks like a nanny goat. (xvi)

Ciardi's discussion of this poem shows his colors as an amateur folklorist and bears quoting in full:

> Billy, Billy, you will recognize of course as a kind of *Georgie Porgie puddin' and pie*. [. . .] Billy, Billy, as nearly as I know, was composed in our fourth-grade schoolyard by a former young poet now in the coal business, and was used to taunt our local sloven who has since washed up, cleaned up, grown up, and joined the police force. Almost inevitably, it earned its young author a punch in the nose—a fair example of the way criticism operates in our society to kill the poetic impulse. (xvi)

Though Ciardi groups "invective" in the category of "bad poetry," he nevertheless "insist[s] that *Billy, Billy*, is not at all bad," a curious contradiction that seems, again, predicated on his use of these poems as devices serving his larger, pedagogical aim—that is, to educate what he calls "the reader of (some) general culture" (244). This reader falls into the "'new class' of salaried managers, administrators, academics, technicians and journalists" that Jackson Lears maintains emerged after World War II, a class of people who "manipulated symbols rather than made things, whose stock in trade consisted of their organizational, technical, conceptual or verbal skills" (50). It is also worth noting that a large percentage of Ciardi's own children's poetry falls into the category of invective, taunting and teasing both his child and adult readers. As X. J. Kennedy writes in "Strict and Loose Nonsense," Ciardi "loves to keep a reader from feeling smug" (229).

This pedagogical impulse is also apparent in Ciardi's poetry for children. If he intended *Mid-Century* to educate and, in Brunner's words, "captur[e] the attention of the general reader," then it seems he intended his children's poetry to enlighten the child (57). In service of this aim Ciardi *domesticates* playground poetry (like "Billy, Billy") by employing it for pedagogical purposes. Unlike Roethke, the style Ciardi employs when writing his adult poetry differs from that employed in his children's poetry. Brunner characterizes Ciardi's style (ignoring his children's poetry) as a "'middle style'—a style that is adjectivally unadorned, restricted to a diction of familiar words, and straightforward in its syntax" (48). Certainly Ciardi's children's poems follow the letter of this characterization—few adjectives and adverbs, simple diction and syntax. However, his use of assonance and consonance, alliterative effects, and playful incorporation of end and internal rhymes in conjunction with surprising use of enjambment are much more flamboyant in his children's poetry, almost as if calling attention to these poetic conventions in order to *teach* his child readers the musical vocabulary of poetic craft. Brunner makes the convincing case that "the conventions of 1950s poetry rarely encouraged and tacitly prohibited verse as an extended expression of pleasure" (181). He quotes James E. B. Breslin's recasting of William Carlos Williams's characterization of the 1950s as the "age of sonnets": "Williams might have been a little more accurate had he declared it the age of the sestina" (qtd. in Brunner 165). The sestina, Brunner argues, "allowed the poet to acknowledge, and even to demonstrate, that the calling to the life of poetry had something to do with a love of language, with the sheer musicality that words always possess" (181). However, Ciardi did not have to turn to the sestina to revel in the "extended expression of pleasure," the "sheer musicality that words always possess." And despite Ciardi's claim that readers of mid-century poetry ought to "come prepared for delight" (xv), he refrains from more overt rhythmic and musical play in his adult poetry, reserving such play for his children's poems.

Ciardi is sometimes overt in his use of the children's poem as primer. For instance, "I Met a Man That Was Playing Games," from *I Met a Man*, is ultimately an introduction to rhyme, emphasizing the playful nature of poetry composition:

> —I met a man that was playing games.
> —What kind of games?
> > —About things and names.
> —How do you play?
> > —He didn't say.
> But from what I heard, it goes this way:
> I pick a rhyme—let's say it's "any"—
> If I say "Spend it," you say *penny.*
> If I say "Girl," then you say *Jenny.*
> If I say "Boy," then you say *Kenny.* (1–8)

Cleverly, Ciardi rhymes even the fractured lines 2 and 3, calling attention to rhyme as an organizing principle of the poem, even as he suggests that poetry is a game "[a]bout things and names," recalling William Carlos Williams's pronouncement, "no ideas but in things." Ciardi echoes Williams in *Mid-Century,* writing, "I do not think it is possible for the poet to control the response to abstract labels. Therefore he must give himself to the perceivable" (249). The poem also embodies (though, again, in the extreme) another of Ciardi's principles of poetry: *"Rhyme (internal as well as line-end) is not an appliquéd ornamentation, but part of the total voice-punctuation of the poem"* (251; italics in the original). It also bears noting that the poet figure in the poem is an adult, from whom the children learn the fun of rhyming. That children have an oral tradition of rhyme largely separate from adult influence is elided by the poem. This elision is indicative of the genre of domesticated playground poetry, which is a kind of playground poetry mediated by adults.

Another poem that overtly calls attention to its structure, while incorporating playground poetry's tendency to mock and tease, is "What Did You Learn at the Zoo":

> What did I learn at the zoo?
> Monkeys look like you.
>
> Some are bald and some have curls,
> But monkeys look like boys and girls.
>
> [. . .]
>
> Gorillas are good, gorillas are bad,
> But all of them look a lot like Dad.
>
> Some do one thing, some another,
> But all of them scream a lot like Mother.
>
> What did *we* learn at the zoo?
> Just what we wanted to:
>
> That it's fun to tease if you make it rhyme
> (Though you mustn't do it all the time)[.] (1–4, 9–16)

This poem, included in *You Read to Me, I'll Read to You*, is typical of Ciardi's teasing voice, ridiculing both children and adults, even as it foregrounds form. The last line, for instance, highlights its cleverness by *not* rhyming, answering the question "What did *we* learn at the zoo" with: "that a bottle of lemon-and-lime / Is a very good way to spend a dime. // (And so is a bag of peanuts)" (18–20). As monkeys have a penchant for peanuts, the narrator's parenthetical suggests that he may also have something in common with monkeys, and that perhaps it is also "fun to tease" (or at least to self-depre-cate) without rhyme.

Roethke was also an educator, but his poetry seems less a teasing primer aimed at the young than an embracing of the young, or at least his concept of the child reader. Ciardi reserved the elements of nursery and playground poetry for his children's poetry, whereas Roethke used them in his work for both children and adults. Ever serious about children's rhymes, Roethke consistently treated them as ends in and of themselves, unlike Ciardi, whose use of "Hickory Dickory" and "Billy, Billy" was at the ser-vice of a larger argument about mid-century poetry. Roethke's essay "Some Remarks on Rhythm" analyzes several nursery rhymes, showing great sen-sitivity and thoughtfulness, even to the degree that he carefully explains why one version of a nursery rhyme may not be as successful as another. "Anonymous is my favorite author," Roethke famously wrote in his note-books (*Straw for the Fire* 251). No doubt he was sincere. Roethke explores in "Some Remarks" the profound influence folk rhythms have had on his and other contemporary poetry. Unfortunately, his praise of anonymous litera-ture obscures the communal element that is so central to the production of folk texts of this type, constructing anonymous texts in terms of the literary tradition.[7] In his discussion of folk poetry's influence, Roethke quotes one of his favorite jump-rope rhymes:

> I.N. spells IN.
> I was in my kitchen
> Doin' a bit of stitching.
> Old Father Nimble
> Came and took my thimble.
> I got a great big stone,
> Hit him on the belly-bone.
> O.U.T. spells OUT. (64)

After a brief but telling formal analysis of the piece, one not failing to suggest a possible Freudian interpretation, Roethke then turns to his own poem, "I Need, I Need," which, though definitely rooted in the literary rather than the oral tradition, is nonetheless influenced by playground rhymes.

Roethke notes that "I Need, I Need" contains "a jump-rope section in which two children chant in alternate aggressive dialogue" ("Some Re-marks" 66):

> Even steven all is less:
> I haven't time for sugar,
> Put your finger in your face,
> And there will be a booger. (66)

The next quatrain more obviously borrows from skip-rope rhymes:

> A one is a two is
> I know what you is:
> You're not very nice—
> So touch my toes twice. (66)

The poem continues, growing more and more aggressively nonsensical. Despite the Victorian roots of this nonsense and his limericks' obvious debt to Lear, Roethke's work, adult and children's, is, as Thomas Travisano notes in *Midcentury Quartet,* considerably "more romantic" than that of many of his contemporaries (19).[8] Yet Roethke is a romantic who appreciates the darker side of childhood as well as the light, a tendency that is common in later urchin poetry. Rather than looking to the poetry of childhood for innocence and purity, Roethke understands, as he puts it, childhood's "vagaries, its ambiguous loyalties, its special poignance" (*On the Poet* 105). Preoccupied with what Travisano calls "the wonder and darkness of childhood," Roethke's work suggests something that John Morgenstern makes explicit in "The Fall into Literacy and the Rise of the Bourgeois Child"—namely, that "children [. . .] could be said to create their own literature before one is created for them" (137). Roethke understands this, listens closely to at least one tradition of child-created literature, imitates it, and gives it back to children and adults in the form of his books. Morgenstern suggests that "it might be useful [. . .] to consider to what extent the rhetoric of children's literature is influenced by the rhetoric of children's play" (137). Roethke appears to have already considered this issue. In his case, it is not only his children's poetry that is influenced by the rhetoric of children's play, but his adult poetry as well. In this respect Roethke differs profoundly from Ciardi, whose pedagogical impulse suggests that children need to learn about rhyme and other poetic techniques from adults.

Even Roethke's teasing poems seem to be not so much "invective" as surrealist insights into the child's world with its fears and anxieties, a conception of the child's world emerging from the folk traditions of nursery and playground rhymes. "Dirty Dinky," for example, ends tauntingly (and hauntingly) with a direct address to the child reader that differs considerably from the addresses found in Ciardi's work:

You'd better watch the things you do,
You'd better watch the things you do,
You're part of him; he's part of you
—*You* may be Dirty Dinky. (17–20)

Rife with the "appeals to the unconsciousness, to the fears and desires that go far back into our childhood" that Roethke writes of in "Some Remarks on Rhythm" (71), "Dirty Dinky" achieves the type of evocativeness apparent in one of his favorite nursery rhymes:

Hinx, minx, the old witch winks!
The fat begins to fry!
There's nobody home but Jumping Joan,
And father, and mother, and I.

Consider the second and third stanzas of "Dirty Dinky":

Suppose you walk out in a Storm,
With nothing on to keep you warm,
And then step barefoot on a Worm
        —Of course, it's Dirty Dinky.

As I was crossing a hot hot Plain,
I saw a sight that caused me pain,
You asked me before, I'll tell you again:
        —It *looked* like Dirty Dinky.[9] (5–12)

Like "Hinx, Minx," "Dirty Dinky" erupts from what Roethke calls "the wild disordered language of the natural heart" (*On the Poet* 160). This Dionysian exuberance is certainly more romantic than Victorian, quite obscure, and typically modern, especially if we accept Jarrell's thesis that modern poetry is a continuation of romantic tendencies.[10] In this case, the tendency is Roethke's "passion for 'pure' poetry, for putting everything in terms of sensation and emotion, with logic and generalizations excluded" ("End of the Line" 79).

Roethke's children's poetry—and, indeed, some of Ciardi's—has been criticized for this obscurity and for what some have called a morbid, often violent, sense of humor, the latter reminiscent of playground poetry. "Dirty Dinky" recalls lines in Roethke's villanelle "The Waking":

> Light takes the Tree; but who can tell us how?
> The lowly worm climbs up a winding stair;
> I wake to sleep and take my waking slow. (10–12)

"Dirty Dinky"'s evocative impossibilities like "O what's the weather in a Beard? / It's windy there, and rather weird," seem equally at home in poems like "Unfold! Unfold!":

> Later, I did and I danced in the simple wood.
> A mouse taught me how, I was a happy asker.
> Quite-by-chance brought me many cookies.
> I jumped in butter.
> Hair had kisses. (34–38)

This obscurity is not as common in later urchin poetry, which seems to prefer the straightforward, humorous nonsense of Roethke's limericks ("There once was a cow with a double udder") or the taunting teases of Ciardi's verses. In this respect Roethke and Ciardi anticipated (and perhaps paved the way for) Shel Silverstein and Jack Prelutsky. Silverstein and Prelutsky avoid the obscurist tendencies in both Ciardi and Roethke, the Dionysian experimentation, and, for Ciardi, the pedagogical subtext, but neither balks at featuring violence and ill-mannered children in his poems. Ciardi's and Roethke's success, coupled with their interest in the folk tradition, in playground poetry, nursery rhymes, and their insistence on including violence and unpleasantness, created the environment in which subsequent children's poets could thrive. Silverstein's first book of poetry, *Where the Sidewalk Ends,* coincides with the 1974 publication of Rosen's *Mind Your Own Business,* and *Sidewalk,* alongside Prelutsky's *The New Kid on the Block* (1984), can be viewed as the U.S. version of urchin poetry, dominating the nation's children's poetry sales. Indeed, if *Mind Your Own Business* marks the beginning of urchin poetry in England, just as Dennis Lee's *Garbage Delight* exemplifies urchin poetry in Canada, then *Sidewalk* marks not the beginning of urchin poetry in the United States, but rather a *continuation* of the line begun by Ciardi and Roethke, who form the bedrock on which Silverstein's success was built.

Silverstein and Prelutsky both come from the folk tradition, their work rooted in folk music. As Prelutsky notes in an interview with Karin Snelson, "I knew [Silverstein] before either of us had ever written any children's poems, when we were both in Greenwich Village in the late '50s and early '60s. He was already a legendary character. He had written for *Stars and Stripes* and was doing work for *Playboy,* so he had developed an adult audience. We were both involved with the folk music scene in Greenwich Village" (qtd. in Snelson n.p.). As discussed, Roethke "'sang' several songs,—settings of 'children's' poems" in New York City in the early '50s (*Letters* 189). Unfortunately, we have no recordings of Roethke's performance, but his linking of children's verse to song recalls the melodic elements of playground poetry. Thus Roethke anticipates Silverstein's linking of children's verse to folk and rock music, particularly in Silverstein's LP versions of *Where the Sidewalk Ends* (1984) and *A Light in the Attic* (1985), the former winning him a Grammy for best children's album. As Ruth MacDonald notes, "One can imagine that a poet who comes to written verse from writing rock and roll or blues lyrics is more used to composing and revising out loud than drafting and redrafting on paper" (66).

Unlike Ciardi and Roethke, Silverstein and Prelutsky both compose poetry primarily for children, although Silverstein has produced a great deal of work for adults in a wide variety of forms.[11] This fact alone separates them from their predecessors. John Rowe Townsend's comment that urchin poetry eschews "social or literary pretension" (300) holds true for Silverstein and Prelutsky, perhaps to a greater degree than it does for Roethke and Ciardi. Ciardi, after all, was dedicated to expanding poetry's general audience, and much of his children's poetry works toward that end, whereas the seriousness with which Roethke worked within the playground and nursery rhyme traditions in his adult and children's poetry suggests that he viewed both as literary, if not pretentious. However, although Prelutsky and Silverstein rarely evince these literary pretensions, and although they are very much rooted in oral performance, particularly in that they often sing their poems to guitar accompaniment, they are nonetheless aware of the socializing function of poetry and are not above moralizing.[12] The title poem of *The New Kid on the Block* is a "social" poem of sorts about the titular new kid who, among other bad deeds, "swipe[s]" the narrator's ball (14). The poem ends with a somewhat lame surprise, as we find that the new kid, as bad as bad can be, is actually a girl: "that new kid's really bad, / I don't care for her at all" (15–16). None of the descriptions are very compelling (though line 14 has a certain naughty charm, especially when considering the bully's gender), and the poem turns on its surprising last line, hinging, in fact, on that one element of surprise. Myra Cohn Livingston argues in her 1986 review of *A Light in the Attic* that much of Silverstein's oeuvre is equally moralizing, and points to "Jimmy Jet and His TV Set" (36), in which a child who watches too much TV eventually turns into one, as the epitome of this tendency. I would add that such moralizing is diametrically opposed to the spirit of playground poetry. When it finds its way into their collections, invariably it is to their diminishment.

Like Ciardi's pedagogical emphasis and Roethke's formal preoccupations, such moralizing is a symptom of the *domestication* of playground poetry. Domesticated playground poetry is framed by both the nursery rhyme and playground poetry traditions, but adults outside of childhood mediate it, adults who view childhood through the lens of often fairly conventional ideological preconceptions. Prelutsky's "Jellyfish Stew" is framed by the same gross-out tradition that frames Roethke's "Goo-girl":

> Jellyfish stew,
> I'm loony for you[.]
> [. . .]
> You're soggy, you're smelly,
> you taste like shampoo,
> you bog down my belly
> with oodles of goo[.] (1, 9–12)

Though "Jellyfish Stew" does not have the added dimension of intertextuality found in "Goo-girl" (the narrator of which, Myrtle, is found in two other poems), it arises from the same tradition, a tradition to which Prelutsky's "Ah! A Monster's Lot Is Merry" similarly belongs. This poem features a nasty (in both senses of the word) monster who is "free to be offensive, / free to frolic, free to romp," and free, of course, to make "nauseating noises" (3, 4, 7). He and Roethke's Goo-girl would certainly get along.

A hyperbolic narrative celebrating the unclean and low, Silverstein's "The Dirtiest Man in the World," from *Where the Sidewalk Ends,* involves a "musty and dusty and patchy and scratchy" speaker who, in addition to being "mangy and covered with mold," lives in a pig pen with a menagerie of beasts: five hogs, a chicken, and "three squizzly lizards" (7–8, 12). Another poem, "Warning," incorporates a perennial topic of playground poetry into a mock-cautionary tale that tells of "a sharp-toothed snail" who lives inside our noses: "So," the speaker warns, "if you stick your finger in, / He may bite off your nail" (2–4). Although the print version may seem serious in its didacticism, the illustration accompanying the poem (featuring a boy with his finger buried in his nose) undercuts the morality with gross-out humor. Furthermore, Silverstein's 1984 Grammy award–winning LP version of the book features an alternate ending, one colored with Silverstein's trademark raucous laughter: "So . . . that's why . . . always use your handkerchief. That's right. [pause] / You just take your handkerchief, wrap it around your finger / And jam it up in there." The moral is no longer do not pick your nose, but, rather, do not pick your nose without taking the proper precautions.

Like Ciardi, Silverstein turns the aggressive humor of playground po-
etry back on the child, a strategy he employs in "The Worst," a poem "of
scariness, / Of bloodiness and hairyness" (1–2), which ends with the nar-
rator informing the child reader that the Glurpy Slurpy Skakagrall—obvi-
ously a frightening, child-eating monster—is "Standing right behind" her
(7). Although these poems employ elements of the carnivalesque discussed
in chapter 3, they do so only to a point, and this point, ironically enough, is
one set by the social codes of the dominant culture in which they were pro-
duced. For instance, Silverstein's "Crazy Dream," from *Falling Up* (1996),
is a recounting of a dream in which the child speaker is in charge of his
school. The poem describes a child who has "laid down the rules," rules
that, in carnivalesque fashion, turn the tables on adult authority. It insists
that if the *teacher* talks in class, she will get "pinched" until she cries (4,
18). It also suggests that if she fails to answer ludicrous questions correctly
("If you had seven apples and you gave me three how many teeth would a
canary have?") she, as the illustration makes clear, will be hung by her ears
on a clothesline. However, as rough, rowdy, and resistant as this poem is,
it, like the rest of Silverstein's children's poems, is still bounded by the rules
of the adult culture in which his books are bought and sold, the rules of
the households in which they are read. Ultimately, it is a less violent version
of such common playground rhymes as "Glory, Glory, Hallelujah," which
begins:

> Glory, glory, hallelujah!
> Teacher hit me with a ruler.
> I hid behind the door
> With a loaded .44
> And she ain't my teacher no more!

It is also quite similar to "Mine Eyes Have Seen the Glory":

> Mine eyes have seen the glory of the burning of the school,
> We have beaten every teacher, we have broken every rule!
> We have smashed up all the blackboards, we have thrown out all
>   the books.
> The school is burning down.

"Crazy Dream" features no loaded .44's; it involves no burning schools,
just as it does not describe child revolutionaries who have "tortured every
teacher" and "broken every rule," or have "shot the secretary and hung the

principal." Hanging a teacher by her ears is, at worst, a mild form of torture, and that is as violent as things generally get in Silverstein's children's poetry. There is no shooting, no arson, only pinching. The same is true of both Ciardi's and Roethke's poems, of all domesticated playground poetry. The market demands such domestication.

However, Silverstein does not hesitate to employ profanity, violence, and direct sexual references in his poetry and songs for adults, although, as we've seen, he polices these aspects in his work for children, sweetening his collections with sentimental poems like "Hug o' War," in which the narrator prefers hugs to tugs, because in a hug of war "everyone cuddles, / and everyone wins" (10–11).[13] One of his adult collections, originally appearing in *Playboy,* was republished as *Uncle Shelby's ABZ Book: A Primer for Tender Young Minds* (1961). Because of his later success as a children's author, the *ABZ Book* was reprinted in 1985 with a slight cover change. Though "*A Primer for Tender Young Minds*" still appears on the title page, on the cover the subtitle reads, "*A Primer for Adults Only,*" the back cover insisting, "The notorious early Silverstein classic you won't want your children to read." This, of course, is as much of an enticement as it is a warning, using our preconceptions about the innocence of children's writers to titillate and intrigue, propagating Silverstein's bad-boy persona. Furthermore, it ties the children's author back to the playboy who authored such gems as "Quaaludes Again" and "I Love My Right Hand," songs that sound much more like playground poetry than many of the poems Silverstein wrote with an actual child audience in mind. Another of his adult works that seems as if it could have emerged from the playground is his relentlessly sacrilegious ballad "The Devil and Billy Markham," a poem that first appeared in *Playboy's* January 1979 issue. This poem is so outrageous that I hesitate to quote any of the sections that would support this claim (it does appear in its entirety on www.banned-width.com, however, and I direct the curious reader there). These works, along with some of his other adult songs, "Fuck 'Em" and "I Got Stoned and I Missed It," for instance, also have more similarities to playground poetry than to his children's poetry.[14]

Thus, when MacDonald argues that Silverstein's children's poems encourage children to become producers of poetry, we have to wonder what kind of poems it encourages them to produce. She points to "Invitation," the opening poem in *Sidewalk,* as a piece that urges "child readers to be storytellers themselves as well as to join in the experience of the others' tales" (33). This may be true, but the kind of poetry it encourages children to partake in, to produce, holds little of the impassionedly resistant qualities of playground poetry or, arguably, its formal complexity or striking images. Indeed, neither Silverstein nor Prelutsky seems to recognize that child culture *already* produces, disseminates, and reimagines a poetic tradition much like his own, but with a sharper edge. Undoubtedly their publishers recognize who purchases poetry for children—namely, parents—and thus package and market their books for this buying public. Although Silverstein's books are available only in hardcover and are quite expensive, it is unlikely that parents will ever buy their children the soft-cover and less expensive *Greasy Grimy Gopher Guts* as an alternative.[15] Unlike the verse of official school poetry, domesticated playground poetry—the literary, adult-produced analog to playground poetry—often offers little that is new to child culture besides an adult-controlled replacement.

Roethke's *I Am! Says the Lamb* is perhaps an exception to what I'm describing. Throughout the collection Roethke's rigorous exploration of the nursery rhyme and playground poetry tradition is evident, as is his desire to supplement that tradition with his own stylistic inventions. Unlike Ciardi, who in poems like "I Met a Man" seeks to teach children poetic techniques, Roethke, in "Myrtle" (the companion piece for "Goo-girl" and "Myrtle's Cousin") shows an awareness that the young have their own tradition and are in the position to be quite severe critics. "Myrtle" also demonstrates Roethke's respect for the child reader as well as the child poet, as it contains a disorienting intertextuality and self-reflexivity. The speaker is the poet, telling of a turtle who critiques the very book we hold in our hands. He tells of a "girl named Myrtle / Who [. . .] could growl like a Bear" (1, 2, 4). "*Nobody understood*" her, the poem continues, concluding (5):

> She would sit with a Book on her Knees—
> *My* Poetry-Book, if you please—
> She'd Rant and She'd Roar:
> "This stuff is a Bore!
> Why I could do better
> With only ONE Letter—
> These Poets, they write like *I* Sneeze!" (6–12)

The first stanza is a conventional limerick. However, the second stanza significantly departs from the limerick form, adding a dimetrical couplet at the center. This departure calls attention to the poem's theme—the inadequacy of the poetry Myrtle is reading, the poetry, perhaps, of "Nonsense Poems," the first section of *I Am!* and perhaps the inadequacy of domesticated playground poetry in general. The poetry is "a Bore" precisely because it is defanged, because it does not contain, as rough as it may be, the razor edge and uncompromising language of the playground. Furthermore, Myrtle's comment "These Poets, they write like *I* Sneeze!" suggests the bodily, carnivalesque elements that are so common in playground poetry: her sneeze is equal to the writing of the poets of the literary tradition, whose work finds its way into bound books like the one she reads. Myrtle's nonsensical claim that she "could do better / With only ONE letter" makes perfect sense if we consider that her poetry could be oral poetry, which needs no letters at all. The capitalized "ONE" calls attention to the oral performance of her words, highlighting that the last bit of the poem is a score for voice, part of the oral tradition.

As opposed to Prelutsky, Ciardi, and Silverstein, Roethke does not limit himself to the domesticated playground poetry paradigm. Silverstein's work departs from the oral tradition through the original use of visual layout and interaction between image and word, a departure that is common in domesticated playground poetry and one that places him solidly in the tradition of poet/illustrators like Edward Lear and Heinrich Hoffman. Yet Silverstein nonetheless writes *exclusively* domesticated playground poetry. Roethke, on the other hand, includes his "Greenhouse Poems" in *I Am! Says the Lamb,* confirming his desire to provide children with a multifarious view of what poetry can be. He does not condescend to children, does not assume that they are interested only in nonsense and light verse. Rather, he offers them options. Beatrice Roethke expanded on these options in 1973 when she released *Dirty Dinky and Other Creatures,* a collection containing excerpts from "Where Knock Is Open Wide," "I Need, I Need," "The Lost Son," and "The Long Waters," in addition to many domesticated playground poems and the aforementioned "Greenhouse" poems. This sort of stylistic diversity is rare in single author collections.

Unfortunately, all three of Roethke's children's books have long been out of print. And while some of Ciardi's books do remain in print, one gets the feeling that their association with Edward Gorey's illustrations takes the credit for their shelf life, as Ciardi's children's books illustrated by others are largely unavailable. However, even those Ciardi books that remain in print are rarely stocked in most of the larger chain bookstores. Silverstein and Prelutsky, however, are amply represented. As Anita Tarr notes in "Nonsense Now," Shel Silverstein's "works are often the only ones young children are exposed to" (86). With his *Random House Book of Poetry for Children* (1983) and scores of individual collections, Jack Prelutsky is no doubt on par with Silverstein in popularity. These two poets are not simply the most famous authors of *urchin poetry* in the United States; they are also the most famous writers of *children's poetry* in the United States. It behooves us, then, to remember that these two giants of U.S. children's poetry are situated in a tradition that stretches back to Ciardi's and Roethke's midcentury dissatisfaction with mainstream children's poetry, a tradition that borrows from, participates in, and in some ways resists an even older tradition. Domesticated playground poetry is charged with the tension between its carnivalesque roots and its adult authors' desire to self-censor, to teach, to experiment, to sell product. It is charged with the interplay between its oral foundations and its current print form, its subversive impulses, and the tempering of those impulses by the industry that markets and sells it. Because this poetry is so tightly braided to both the folk poetry many children recite and circulate among themselves and the literary poetry that is produced and distributed by adults, critics should resist dismissing domesticated playground poetry. This poetry and the competing interests and varied social moments in which it is produced deserve to be discussed as the complex and exciting subjects they are.

5

A Defense
of Visual Poetry for Children

Come, I'll take no denial;
We must have a trial:
For really this morning I've nothing to do.

Lewis Carroll, "A Mouse's Tale"

A discussion of children's poetry written in the United States after the mid-century would be incomplete without acknowledging visual poetry, a rich but often misunderstood art form. Just as the academic establishment all but ignores visual poetry for adults (or as members of the post-avant movements of the late twentieth and early twenty-first centuries call it, "vispo"), so too academics who are interested in contemporary children's literature ignore visual poetry for children. For instance, in her groundbreaking work on children's poetry, *From the Garden to the Street* (1998), Morag Styles avoids any discussion of visual poetry whatsoever. She does, as we saw in chapter 4, touch on urchin poetry, a form of verse that we might fruitfully align with visual poetry, as they are both irresponsibly maligned, existing—thriving even—in a fairly "hostile critical climate" (Styles 263). This hostility precludes a full assessment of urchin poetry's aesthetic potential. Similarly, the hostility surrounding visual poetry has clouded our view of the art form while blinding us to its complex history. In this chapter I seek to situate visual poetry for children in the context of avant-garde visual poetry for adults in North America and the world. In so doing, I hope to suggest the promise and the limitations of visual poetry, while clearing up some of the common misconceptions about this type of poetry that are shared by both academics and laypeople.

Visual poetry in English-language children's literature stepped into the spotlight in the 1860s, with Lewis Carroll's famous pair of mouse poems.[1] In the United States, however, visual poetry—for children and for adults—entered into the public eye at a much later date and since that date has encountered quite stalwart resistance. It was not until the late 1960s and early 1970s that visual poetry began to be recognized as a literary movement of any consequence, primarily through the publication of two landmark anthologies for adults, Emmett Williams's *An Anthology of Concrete Poetry* (1967) and Mary Ellen Solt's *Concrete Poetry: A World View* (1968). Shortly thereafter, Robert Froman, whose work, like Carroll's, demonstrates a preoccupation with math, logic, and puzzles, wrote some of the earliest visual poetry for children published in the United States, collected in his *Street Poems* (1971) and *Seeing Things: A Book of Poems* (1974). The 1970s showed a boom in visual poetry for children, with even relatively conservative poets like Myra Cohn Livingston trying their hand at visual work, though few critics found occasion to discuss it. To understand the appeal of visual poetry that was written and marketed for children in the latter half of the twentieth century, as well as the general resistance to it, we need to ground this tradition in the context of visual poetry for adults, historicizing both the practice of and resistance to visual poetry for adults.

Dick Higgins's *Pattern Poetry* (1987) makes clear that visual poetry has a long and rich history, though its subtitle, *Guide to an Unknown Literature,* foregrounds the fact that it is often forgotten and misunderstood. Its history does not start with the Dadaists or the Futurists, or even with the typographical experiments of Stéphane Mallarmé or Guillaume Apollinaire. Rather, it stretches back to Hellenistic Greece, perhaps the earliest piece being the "Phaistos Disk," written in Minoan A (vii, 4). Pattern poetry—a name Higgins ascribes to pre–twentieth century visual poetry—generally existed in the margins of poetic discourse, especially in English-speaking cultures. The history of such pattern poetry on the global scale is tangled indeed. However, for our purposes we will concentrate on the English tradition, which is much more manageable. As far as we know, visual poetry in English began in the late 1500s, Richard Willis's poetry being the earliest to survive (Higgins 96). Modeled closely on Hellenistic Greek pattern poetry (the models taken from the medieval "Greek Anthology"), pattern poems of this period often employ "axes, altars, eggs, wings, syrinxes, [. . .] [and] a handful of other approved forms" (Higgins 95). Unlike shaped poems of the twentieth century, which are marked by exceptional originality of shape and a fixation on formal experimentation and innovation, early English pattern poems are characterized by "formal conservatism," poets rarely deviating from the forms first used by their Greek forebears (Higgins 36). Even George Herbert and Robert Herrick, who have written perhaps the most famous pattern poems in English, limited themselves to prescribed forms.

Herbert and Herrick wrote during what is arguably the high point of English-language pattern poetry, but even then critics attacked the form, as Higgins demonstrates. For example, Gabriel Harvey, in his letters to Spenser (1580), writes that pattern poetry is written by "folishe idle, phantasticall poet[s] (and deviser[s])" (qtd. in Higgins, *Pattern Poetry* 14). Harvey, like subsequent twentieth-century critics, complains that "Nothinge so absurde and fruteles but being once taken upp shall have sume imitatoures" (14). In the seventeenth century John Dryden exemplifies highbrow disdain for visual poetry, writing in his mock-epic *Macflecknoe* (1682):

> Thy genius calls then not to purchase fame
> In keen iambics, but mild anagram:
> Leave writing plays, and choose for thy command
> Some peaceful province in Acrostic Land.
> There thou may'st wings display and altars raise,
> And torture one poor word ten thousand ways. (203–08)

Considering the prevalence of wing- and altar-shaped poems in the sixteenth and seventeenth centuries, it remains unclear whether Dryden is mocking specifically Herbert's famous poems "Altar" and "Easter Wings," the first stanza of which appears thus:

> Lord, who createdst man in wealth and store,
> Though foolishly he lost the same,
> Decaying more and more,
> Till he became
> Most poor:
> With thee
> Oh let me rise
> As larks, harmoniously,
> And sing this day thy victories:
> Then shall the fall further the flight in me.[2] (1–10)

What is certain, however, is Dryden's vitriol concerning shaped poems. Dryden's view on pattern poetry was not uncommon, and by the time neoclassical tastes ascended in the late seventeenth century, pattern poetry written in English had fallen completely out of vogue. By the eighteenth century it had disappeared entirely. Visual poetry did not return until the Victorian period, at which time most pattern poets wrote anonymously, save the notable exception of Charles Dodgson (who, incidentally, wrote under a pseudonym).

Just as visual poetry is not new, the United States' resistance or ambivalence to visual poetry for children and adults is not new. Apollinaire's visual experiments in France were recognized in the United States by avant-gardists like Ezra Pound (who was the first American to refer to Apollinaire's *Alcools* in print), but most reviewers and critics disregarded as a fad both Apollinaire's simultanism movement and literary cubism. A notable exception was Marius de Zayas, whose avant-garde journal *291*, launched in March 1915, showcased Apollinaire's theory of simultanism. As a variation of literary cubism, simultanism championed visual poetry as a viable method of constructing texts simulating, in de Zayas's words, "the polyphony of simultaneous voices which say different things" (qtd. in Bohn, *Apollinaire* 51). Perhaps more germane to the discussion here, simultanism is a method of constructing texts that were "simultaneously painting and poem" and thus "communicated on two different levels at the same time" (52). This tension between vocal polyphony and mixed media is still prevalent in U.S. visual poetry, especially, as we shall see, in those works that are composed and marketed for children: collage and mixed-media art more often than not accompany the visual poem.

Besides de Zayas's caricatures and Apollinaire's work, *291* published other visual works, notably "A Bunch of Keys" by U.S. poet J. B. Kerfoot, a poem that exemplifies the successful balancing of the visual and the verbal.

A quick analysis of this poem will serve us later in the analysis of visual poems for children, both successful and unsuccessful. Here we see Kerfoot burlesquing the bourgeois life, a life that Willard Bohn reminds us Kerfoot participated in. Bohn writes, "[Kerfoot's] was a life that revolved about the office and the home and was characterized by repeated indulgence in good cigars, fine wines, expensive items such as jewelry, and sex" (*Modern* 131). Bohn points out that the opening of the poem suggests that Kerfoot realizes he is "chain[ed]" by these appetites and argues that the poem is "intended as a humorous self-portrait," one that encourages us "to examine our own key rings to see what they tell us about ourselves" (131). Yet we might add that the visual dimension of the poem, the surface *look* of the poem, emphasizes the attractiveness of the material possessions enumerated in the piece, even as its circular pattern stresses the vicious cycle of consumption. Furthermore, the poem implicates readers—even those who might resist the bourgeois lifestyle—in Baudelairean fashion. We, like Baudelaire's hypocrite reader, are Kerfoot's double, for we "wish / [we] / knew" what hidden pleasures might be unlocked by that last key, that last curious line of verse.

Despite William Innes Homer's praise that "in design and content there was no periodical in America more advanced than *291*," the journal lasted only one year (194). However, as Bohn reminds us, it lasted long enough to attract the ire of Amy Lowell, who, anticipating future resistance to visual poetry and following in a long tradition of detractors, calls Apollinaire's calligrams and, by extension, visual poetry as a whole, an "extreme fad." Lowell continues, labeling the simultanism movement "'Fantaisisme,' with Guillaume Apollinaire as the chief priest, who wrote so-called 'ideographic poetry,' or poems printed so as to represent a picture of a railroad train with puffing smoke, or some other thing of the sort. That these 'notions' [. . .] will survive the war is inconceivable" (qtd. in *Apollinaire* 56). Inconceivable or not, these notions did survive the war and have been finding their way into children's poetry for the last thirty-five years.

Since Lowell, traditionalists have similarly demonstrated a distrust of experimental, visual work. For instance, in a scathing review of Jerome Rothenberg and George Quasha's rather progressive *America: A Prophecy* (1973), Helen Vendler critiques the anthology for contributing to the wholesale hijacking of our children's poetic education. She insists, "American children no longer read any poetry to speak of in the schools," continuing, "with Chaucer, Shakespeare, Milton, Wordsworth, Keats and Whitman not yet given to them, are they to read Pawnee Bear Songs and Dadaist experiments, aleatory 'art' and Hoodoo chants?" (7).[3] No doubt Vendler would be more accepting of Harold Bloom's 2002 collection, *Stories and Poems for Extremely Intelligent Children of All Ages,* in which Bloom argues, "If readers are to come to Shakespeare and to Chekhov, to Henry James and to Jane

Austen, then they are best prepared if they have read Lewis Carroll and Edward Lear, Robert Louis Stevenson and Rudyard Kipling" (21). Bloom laments that "Children's Literature [. . .] now all too often is a mask for the dumbing-down that is destroying our literary culture. Most of what is now commercially offered as children's literature would be inadequate fare for any reader of any age at any time" (15–16). As seen in the previous chapter, Myra Cohn Livingston makes comparable complaints pertaining specifically to children's poetry in her essay "David McCord's Poems: Something Behind the Door." Similarly appealing to higher cultural interests, Livingston rails against what she characterizes as an assault on children's literature: "The country literally crawls with those who would engage us in worship of the incoherent, the urban scene with its tawdry images, its places of poverty and squalor" (157). This poetry of "idiocy and babbling and the black arts," she maintains, has "until recent times [. . .] managed to confine itself to those who are old enough to choose their reading from the San Francisco beats, the New York School of pseudo-surrealism, the midwest poets, the confessionalists, and the imagists, or to those who dabble in the Concrete and Found, and who attack the Academics with fury" (157). After such a litany we must wonder what poetry is left. Livingston seems to leave room only for the mid-century nature poem exemplified by the work of David McCord, Robert Frost, and their followers, the poetry of the classroom, rooted in the academic verse of the 1950s.[4]

Visual poetry exists in the liminal space between graphic design, poetry, and visual art; at its most compelling it is, according to Higgins, "intermedial" (*Horizons* 15). Unlike opera, in which libretto, music, stagecraft, and theater remain conceptually distinct, visual poetry operates as a fusion, a conceptual blending of "visual art and literature" (15). In his introduction to *The Aesthetics of Visual Poetry,* Bohn argues that "the creative artist functions best in a challenging atmosphere and that whatever serves as a challenge is legitimate" (1). In essence, he argues for revolutionary, experimental poetic practices, the very practices of many of the poets Livingston decries, poets who, in her words, "dabble in the Concrete and Found" (157). Bohn continues, "By defamiliarizing well-worn modes and habits [. . . visual poetry] sharpens the reader's sensibility and encourages participation in the creation of the poem" (8). Visual poetry at its most interesting tries to reinvent the very act of "reading." It asks for—demands, in fact—participation and dialog with the reader in order for meaning making to occur. Visual poetry generally is a *writerly* endeavor, to borrow from Roland Barthes, as visual poetry tends to wrest control from both the author and the text and places it instead externally, in the gap between artist, text, and reader. Edward Brunner, in his study *Cold War Poetry* (2001), while not turning to

Barthes, clearly describes the readerly text, exemplified by the well-wrought urns of mainstream 1950s poets. In these texts, he writes:

> The reader will be led securely from one point to the next. In this poetry, as in the elaborate plot that unfolds in the course of the mystery novel, the work of integrating the disparate pieces has already been done by the author, and the reader can proceed confidently, knowing the way has been prepared. So carefully has the work been assembled, so elaborately yet professionally, that rereading will only deepen the appreciation. (7)

One of the primary reasons visual poetry has been rejected is because it resists this model and is instead writerly in nature: "the work of integrating the disparate pieces," in Brunner's words, must be done by the reader: the way has not been prepared. As Mary Ellen Solt writes, visual poetry constructs "the new poet-reader" (64), one that Pedro Reis insists "is supposed to help create the poem and accepts the challenge" (296).

Bohn argues that visual poetry also "strives to motivate (or remotivate) the signifier, to restore its fundamental identity as a material object" (*Modern* 16). In this sense, visual poetry is eminently an avant-garde endeavor, for it foregrounds what Marjorie Perloff calls "radical artifice": "Artifice, in this sense, is less a matter of ingenuity and manner [. . .] than of the recognition that a poem or painting or performance text is a *made thing*—contrived, constructed, chosen—and that its reading is also a construction on the part of its audience" (*Radical Artifice* 27–28). Perloff notes, "In the nineteenth century, the 'look' of the poem was largely taken for granted, and the reader was given directions to read from left to right, from top of the page to the bottom. The typographic revolution of modernism changed that forever" ("Yale" 395). As Bohn insists in *Modern Visual Poetry,* "Where visual poetry differs from ordinary poetry is in the extent of its iconic dimension, which is much more pronounced, and in its degree of self-awareness" (15). He continues, "Visual poems are immediately recognizable by their refusal to adhere to a rectilinear grid and by their tendency to flout their plasticity" (15).

Reviewers of children's visual poetry certainly recognize this flouting of plasticity, just as publishers recognize the value in the celebration of the "iconic dimension." Most visual poetry collections for children seem to use the visual aspect of the poetry as a marketing gimmick to set their poetry apart from more conventional fare. Though not referring directly to visual poetry, Megan Tingley, vice president of the Little, Brown imprint Megan Tingley Books, notes that "a book of verse needs to *look* fresh and engaging if it is going to appeal to youngsters" (qtd. in Lodge n.p.). This emphasis on the *look* of poetry collections for children is not new, though the conflation of image and poem into *visual poetry* is. Of course, this raises an important distinction between illustrated collections of poetry and collections of visual poetry. In England, poems found on the earliest battledores (circa the 1750s) were accompanied by image, just as the rhymed alphabets in the various editions of the *New England Primer* (first printed in the 1680s) were adorned by somewhat crude, but nonetheless charming, woodcuts. In fact, the history of children's poetry publication is the history of image and text working synergistically, from the early battledores to Robin Hirsch's visually arresting collection *FEG: Stupid Ridiculous Poems for Intelligent Children* (2002), illustrated by Ha. Though at times the poems within *FEG* verge on visual poetry, more often than not they are simply a continuation of the long history of illustrated poetry texts, Hirsch's poems accentuated by Ha's exceptional art and layout, much as Carl Sandburg's poems are refigured by Istvan Banyai's compelling visual designs in *Poems for Children Nowhere Near Old Enough to Vote* (1999).[5]

However, in their pursuit of a visually engaging book, editors sometimes publish books of poetry that are little more than visually arresting doggerel. For example, J. Patrick Lewis's *Doodle Dandies* (1998), comprised of less-than-successful visual poetry, has nonetheless been praised by reviewers. GraceAnne A. DeCandido's review of *Doodle Dandies* epitomizes the positive reception the book has received, praising the iconic dimension of the poems and claiming, "The 'Skyscraper' shape is elegant if obvious, and the poem called 'Winter' creates a verse of white letters drifting and falling on dark sky as evocatively as any Japanese scroll on silk" (1876). She also notes how the book resists conventional reading habits: "Some of the poems involve turning the book about to read all the words" (1876). However, as shall be seen, Lewis's collection does not utilize the tropes of visual poetry to any compelling effect. Rather, the visual component of the poems functions as a sort of window dressing to make rather pedestrian poems appear more interesting than they are.

Like most collections of visual poetry for children, Lewis's book is largely comprised of calligrams that are more specific and representational in their form than concrete poems, which are more abstract and nonrepresentational. In *This Is Not a Pipe,* Michel Foucault writes that a calligram is a poem "composed of lines delimiting the form of an object while also arranging the sequence of letters. It lodges statements in the space of a shape, and makes the text *say* what the drawing *represents*" (21). Carroll's "A Mouse's Tale" from *Alice's Adventures in Wonderland* is a good example of the calligram:

"Fury said to
         a mouse, That
            he met in the
               house, 'Let
                  us both go
                     to law: *I*
                        will prose-
                           c u t e *you.*
                        Come, I'll
                     take no de-
                  n i a l; We
               m u s t have
            a trial :
         For really
         this morn-
      ing I've
   nothing
   to do.'
Said the
   mouse to
      the cur,
         'Such a
            trial, dear
               Sir, With
                  no jury
                     or judge,
                     w o u l d
                     be wast-
                     ing our
                     breath.'
                  'I' ll be
               j u d g e,
            I'll b e
         j u r y,'
      S a i d
   c u n -
   n i n g
   o l d
      Fu r y
         ' I'll
            t r y
            t h e
               whole
                  cause,
                     a n d
                  c o n -
               demn
            you to
         death.'" (Carroll 37)

The poem is not about a *tail,* the shape that the poem takes, but it is a *tale* revealing the poem's sophistication of visual/homophonic punning. Foucault stresses that the calligram's success lies in its ability to "playfully efface the oldest oppositions of our alphabetical civilization: to show and to name; to shape and to say; to reproduce and to articulate; to imitate and to signify; to look and to read" (22). Part of the humor in Carroll's poem arises from its foregrounding of the disjunctures among spoken language, the written word, and the shapes we can make with those words, *tail, tale,* and the image of a tail. Furthermore, as Donald Gray points out (referencing Gary Graham and Jeffrey Maiden), even when formatted in traditional, rectilinear form, the poem is calligrammatic, each stanza resembling a little anapestic mouse of a tercet (24):

> Come, I'll take no denial;
> We must have a trial:
> For really this morning I've nothing to do.

With their long, trailing third lines (and the resultant wait for that last, dilatory rhyme), each stanza creates a sort of sonic image of itself, as we wait for the third, concluding rhyme to slip around the corner.

However, J. Patrick Lewis's good-humored pieces *simply* efface the opposition between showing and naming. They do not use the confoundment of that opposition to any other effect. Certainly, the text of Kerfoot's "A Bunch of Keys" *says* what its shape *represents,* but the image—the circular form, the extended chain ending in a ring reminiscent of a shackle—provides the reader occasion to create a plurality of sometimes contradictory meanings. The shape of Carroll's poem contradicts the verbal signification of his piece, even as it cleverly mirrors the tangled tale of the mouse; suggests the crooked, self-appointed judge and jury; and enacts the unfortunate twists of fate that seem bent on ending with the mouse's death. J. Patrick Lewis's poems, however, are readerly; they work toward a single reading, and that reading is not complicated or enhanced (other than by simple reiteration) by the image formed by the words.

Take, for example, the poem "Mirror":

Printed behind the traditionally formatted poem is a mixed-media image of a blonde, blue-eyed girl wearing a stocking cap, gazing toward the book's gutter. On the facing page, behind the backward text, is a representation of a mirror, in which we can see the same blonde-haired girl winking. The poem is amusing, making interesting use of line breaks, especially in line 3, the rupturing of "I-/dentical" suggesting the fragmented self of the speaker. The second such fragmentation, in line 7, is more problematic, serving only to maintain the line's syllable count. The addressed "you" in the poem also seems to shift at the end of the poem. In the first two instances "you" most likely refers to the mirror image ("You [the image] are looking out"), while in the third instance it seems to refer to the mirror itself: "When one of you [the mirror] / makes two of me" (9–10). Of course, this "you" could still be read as the reflection, but the ambiguity is not very interesting and reads more like a flaw than productive slipperiness. Thus, the text of the poem is not as compelling as it might be, and the visual dimension seems, again, mere reiteration of the subject: the poem concerns a mirror; therefore the text is mirrored. Beyond that, the visual formatting of the text does not add to or comment on the literal meaning of the poem.

In this respect I can sympathize with Livingston's distrust of visual poetry for children, especially when produced by, in her words, "dabbl[ers]" (Lewis is a much better writer of straight nonsense verse than visual poetry). However, as John Berger writes in *Ways of Seeing* (though he speaks of sixteenth-century oil painting), "Hack work is not the result of either clumsiness or provincialism; it is the result of the market making more insistent demands than the art" (88). The same holds true for visual poetry for children, especially, as in Lewis's case, when the market specifically labels the product as poetry, not simply graphic design (the subtitle of *Doodle Dandies* is *Poems That Take Shape*). Berger elaborates: "[I]t is in this contradiction between art and market that the explanations must be sought for what amounts to the contrast, the antagonism existing between the exceptional work and the average" (88). I have to agree. Lewis's book is flashy, appealing to the sensibility of editors like Megan Tingley who desire books that "*look* fresh and engaging" (my emphasis), regardless of whether the poems *are* fresh and engaging. It is not to these rather flashy collections of poetry that we can look for complicated visual work. Instead, we can turn to anthologies for children and, as argued elsewhere, to more modest collections, such as Arnold Adoff's now out-of-print but exceptionally complex *Slow Dance Heart Break Blues* (1995).[6]

In contrast to Lewis's "Mirror," let us examine one of Adoff's pieces, one we could call "He/She." Fixing this poem with a title is difficult, because it consists of two poems united visually on the page—"He" and its near-mirror image "ehS":

He:	:ehS
There	erehT
is	si
hair	riah
on	no
my	ym
upper	reppu
lip.	.pil

Here Adoff explores the typographic semantics pioneered by the concrete poets. Vacillating between specific and abstract, the poem's visual layout only suggests the image made overt by Lisa Desimini's compelling mixed-media illustrations in *Doodle Dandies*. Superimposed on Desimini's picture of a blonde girl looking at herself in a mirror, Lewis's poem is coupled with the poem's title, "Mirror," which is clearly the subject of the poem. However, rather than constructing a scene with the semantic meaning of the words themselves, or through illustration, or even through the title, Adoff's piece evokes a twofold image solely through typography. The mirrored reflection of the words suggests both a boy and a girl examining their faces in mirrors, perhaps a bathroom mirror similar to William Cotton's collage on the front cover. The poem points to how the same utterance when spoken by different people can have diametrically opposite meanings, how the same "objective" fact has different meanings in different contexts. The boy's observation in the mirror may be a point of pride—and his text is formatted conventionally—while the girl's observation may be cause for dread, even as her text is formatted unconventionally. Foregrounding the insecurity and self-consciousness of two adolescents in a form that resists the structural prescriptions of mainstream verse, the poem encourages teens to resist the cultural prescriptions at the root of their insecurities. Indeed, in the central line of the "ehS" poem is "no," positioned directly above "ym," the abbreviated title of the popular teen fashion and beauty magazine *Young and Modern*. Unlike in Lewis's mirror poem, the reversal of Adoff's text does not simply reiterate the fact that the speakers gaze into a looking glass. Rather, it serves to complicate the poem and provides occasion for writerly reading: when youngsters begin to grow facial hair, they may become interested in sex; females may begin taking the "pil" in line 7, to obsess about fractured "reppu[tations]," as in line 6.

Yet visual poetry may go beyond even Adoff's ingenious manipulations of typography. In "The Marginalization of Poetry," Bob Perelman notes that visual poetry is "immune to standardizing / media: to quote them you need / a photocopier not a word processor" (7). Though he is speaking specifically of the late pages of Charles Olson's *Maximus,* "where the orientation of the lines / spirals more than 360 degrees" his words apply equally to X. J. Kennedy's children's poem "Concrete Cat," which needs a photocopier or digital scanner to be reproduced.

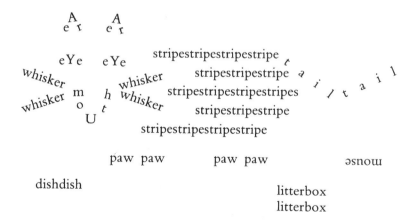

Writing under the pseudonym Dorthi Charles (Kennedy's first name is Charles, and his wife's name is Dorothy), Kennedy intended this poem to parody concrete poetry.[7] "Concrete Cat" first appeared in the second edition of his *An Introduction to Poetry* (1971), and then later appeared in both editions of his and Dorothy Kennedy's anthology for children, *Knock at a Star* (1982 and 1999). According to Kennedy, he wrote the poem for his anthology as an attempt to represent "the sillier kind of concrete poem that simply and unfeelingly arranges words like so many Lincoln Logs" (*Instructor's* 64), poems, perhaps, like those in Lewis's collection.[8] If we remember that the first notable examples of visual poetry for children were Lewis Carroll's mouse poems, we may suspect that the upside-down mouse carries allusive weight, suggesting the death of that tradition, that visual poetry is an aesthetic dead end. However, like Samuel Griswold Goodrich, who in 1846 wrote "Higgledy Piggledy Pop" to demonstrate the worthlessness of Mother Goose, Kennedy was more successful with "Concrete Cat" than he may have intended.[9] Anything but a "poem that simply and unfeelingly arranges words like so many Lincoln Logs," "Concrete Cat," as we will see, illustrates instead the promise of pictorial poetry.

Again, visual poetry at its best foregrounds its materiality, calls attention to the conditions of its production, reminds readers that they are reading a poem, that poems—all poems, not just visual ones—are material objects participating in a poetic tradition. "Concrete Cat," which Kennedy constructed by physically "cut[ting] and past[ing] together" scraps of language (*Instructor's* 64), foregrounds that materiality and asserts its physicality. "Concrete Cat" (ironically, considering Kennedy's poetic conservatism), satisfies Charles Bernstein's call for new, progressive poetry, as presented in "Against National Poetry Month as Such": "The reinvention [of poetry], the making of a poetry for our time, is the only thing that makes poetry matter. And that means, literally, making poetry *matter,* that is[,] making poetry that intensifies the matter or materiality of poetry—acoustic, visual, syntactic, semantic" (n.p.). Kennedy's piece insists upon its nature as a printed, textual artifact. Unlike conventional poems—and even the two mirror poems discussed earlier—Kennedy's cat implies no speaker and so lacks the spoken, aural dimension that is so common in mainstream poetry. In fact, Kennedy resists the conventional wisdom entrenched in mainstream U.S. poetry since the 1950s (that is, poetry written after the experimental push of the first quarter century)—that poems must be representational. As Jed Rasula writes of U.S. mid-century poetry in *American Poetry Wax Museum,* "Poetry was emphatically and resolutely taken to be an art of reference and representation; an art of depiction and assertion. Furthermore, what was asserted in the poem was the articulated intentionality of 'the speaker,' a figure of sensibility, perceptual resourcefulness, and determinate contours" (203). "Concrete Cat" implies no such speaker, sensible or otherwise.

Kennedy is a scion of the representational neo-formalist poets exemplified by Wilbur and Lowell, poets whose work uniformly embraces a poetic of voice. This poem, which, again, intends to mock the concrete tradition, differs from his other work in that it is primarily a *visual* artifact—sound plays little or no role in its meaning-making. As Eugene Wildman writes in *Anthology of Concretism,* "Printed poetry is not like oral poetry; it is not oral poetry set in print. Print is something by itself. [Visual poems] depend for their effect on the special quality of the printed letter and of type spread across a page. It is profoundly literary, for it deals expressly with the effects of writing (as opposed to telling)" (163–64). With traditional, rectilinear poems, readers usually conform to overdetermined reading habits; with "Concrete Cat" we try to take the entire picture in at once and, finding this impossible, have freer rein to travel around the poem's surface in improvisational arcs, to create meaning in ways not rigidly ordained by the writer. Eminently a visual piece, "Concrete Cat" is radical for stressing the difference between sign and signifier, recalling Ferdinand de Saussure, and even more radical in that it, at least to this reader, escapes quite neatly the intention of its writer. The poem speaks to Saussure's pronouncement, "All definitions of words are made in vain" (qtd. in Bohn, *Modern Visual Poetry* 27). Is this poem a pictographic definition of a cat? Does it really look like a cat, or is the resemblance as culturally overdetermined as that between a smiley face "☺" and a human face? "Concrete Cat" highlights the arbitrary link between sign and signifier, poking fun at those, like William and Betty Greenway, who believe that "Words [. . .] are transparent: they allow us to see through to the thing itself" (139). The poem seems to ask us, does "eAr" look like an ear? Or "whisker" look like a whisker? In "The Rejection of Closure" Lyn Hejinian describes a closed text as "one in which all the elements of the work are directed toward a single reading of the work. Each element confirms that reading and delivers the text from any lurking ambiguity" (270). Most voice-lyrics, particularly the mainstream, mid-century poetry characterized by Brunner, are closed, as they generally work toward a single reading.

"Concrete Cat," however, is an open text, like Adoff's poem above. Although the form of "Concrete Cat" would seem to preclude a narrative from being told, it nonetheless does tell a story of sorts, and a scatological one at that, recalling the bawdiness of playground poetry. The story is unconventionally expressed, but it is certainly there: a cat has eaten, or perhaps merely killed, a little mouse. High drama, indeed. But the story has enough holes, enough gaps, to remain ambiguous, open, and thus asks readers to fill in the blanks: why is the dead mouse near the litter box? Did the cat eat the mouse and defecate it? If so, why isn't it *in* the litter box? It appears this concrete cat is not a tame cat, just as visual poetry, perhaps, isn't a tame mode of writing. If we take the mouse as an allusive gesture to Carroll's mouse poems, "Concrete Cat" suggests that visual poetry does not deserve a resting place even as undignified as a litter box. The poem invites readers to create the narrative, to become coproducers of meaning. As an open text, Kennedy's poem, like Adoff's, implicitly argues against conventional textual hierarchy. The poem works against authority, even the authority of the writer and the authority of poetic convention. For example, the most conventional section of the poem is the central five lines: "stripe-stripestripestripe / stripestripestripe." Are the words making up this set of stripes "stripes tripe stripes tripe / stripes tripe stripe"? Because he intended the poem as a parody, it stands to reason that Kennedy is calling his poem and concrete poetry in general "tripe" (in fact, Kennedy writes that "the pun in the cat's middle stripe [tripes] is the only place where the language aspires toward poetry and becomes figurative" [*Instructor's* 64]). However, as an open text the poem resists its author's intention, allowing for other readings: perhaps "tripe" can refer to conventional, rectilinear poems? A poem this playful seems to abet such interpretive leaps, for, as Bohn writes, it "encourage[s] [the reader's] participation in the creation of the poem" (*Aesthetics* 8). Furthermore, the whole poem is "figurative" in a sense, as it is *figured* language—that is, configured, shaped, and arranged—on the page.

Though Kennedy intended this poem to be a farce, it holds up very well when compared to Sharon Creech's similar "My Yellow Dog," which appears in her *Love That Dog* (2001). "My Yellow Dog: By Jack" exemplifies the "sillier kind of concrete poem" that Kennedy lampoons.

In the context of Creech's novel in verse, this poem is supposed to have been written by a young poet named Jack. The poem is playful. For instance, we have the potential sound play at the dog's tail: "tail tail / w o l l e y / wag / wag / wag," and the morphological hiccups possible in the head region: "he EYE ad," for one. However, it does not contain the level of visual punning found in Kennedy's piece: the capital "A" to suggest pointed ears; the placement and shape of the "U" in "mouth" to suggest a tongue; the plot possibilities suggested by the upside-down "mouse." "My Yellow Dog" ultimately fails to utilize the tropes of concrete or visual poetry to any effect beyond simple representation. The reason is simple: Sharon Creech is unaware of those tropes, unaware of traditions of visual poetry.

The poem that inspires Jack to write "Yellow Dog" is S. C. Rigg's "The Apple":

```
                              s
                            t
                          e
                        m
            apple  apple        apple apple
         apple yum apple   yum   apple yum apple
        juicy juicy juicy juicy juicy juicy juicy juicy juicy
         crunchy crunchy crunchy crunchy crunchy crunchy
        red yellow green red yellow green red yellow green red
     apple apple apple apple apple apple apple apple apple apple
     apple  apple apple apple apple apple apple apple apple  apple
     apple  apple apple apple apple  apple apple apple apple  apple
     yum delicious  yum delicious yum delicious yum delicious  yum
    yum yum yum yum yum yum yum yum yum yum yum yum yum
    yum yum yum yum yum yum yum yum yum yum yum yum yum
    yum yum yum yum yum yum yum yum yum yum yum yum yum
     yum yum yum yum yum yum wormy worm yuk  yuk  yum yum
     yum yum yum yum yum yum wormy worm  yuk  yuk yum yum
      yum yum yum yum yum yum yum yum yum yum yum yum
       yum delicious yum delicious yum delicious yum delicious
        apple apple apple apple apple apple apple apple apple
         apple apple apple apple apple apple apple apple
          apple apple apple apple apple apple apple
           red yellow green red yellow green red
            crunchy crunchy crunchy crunchy
              juicy juicy juicy juicy
                apple apple
```

Like *Dorthi Charles,* S. C. *Rigg* is a pseudonym, this time for (S)haron (C)reech, *Rigg* being derived from the surname of her husband, Lyle Rigg.

Sharon Creech mentions how visual poetry found its way into the book: "In the story, Jack refers to a poem shaped like an apple and a poem shaped like a house. When I finished the book, I wanted to include poems that Jack refers to, but I hadn't ever seen a poem shaped like an apple or a house. And so I wrote one. That's the Apple Poem in the back of the book, and S. C. Rigg is another of my names" ("Inspiration" n.p.). This passage explains the lack of sophistication in both "The Apple" and "My Yellow Dog." Creech is obviously unfamiliar with visual poetry and its history, unfamiliar with its tropes and possibilities. One of the most important concrete poets, Reinhard Döhl, wrote a poem quite similar to Creech's "The Apple" in 1965, called "Pattern Poem with an Elusive Intruder":

Made popular by Emmett Williams's *Anthology of Concrete Poetry,* this poem has also been included in Paul B. Janeczko's exceptional anthology of visual poems for children, *A Poke in the I* (2001), released the same year as Creech's *Love That Dog.* Unfortunately, Creech appears to be unaware of this poem.

It is with Janeczko's *A Poke in the I* that I would like to end, for, though it does have its limitations (in an anthology of thirty poems by twenty-four poets, five are by Robert Froman), the collection treats visual poetry responsibly, with attention to its history, its tropes, and its sense of play. On the copyright page, for instance, the text is configured to resemble the copyright symbol, the notes page features lines of text exploding from a saxophone, and, perhaps too obviously, the table of contents is shaped like a table, upon which sit sketches of Janeczko and Chris Raschka, the illustrator. The synergy between Raschka's multimedia collage work and the various poems selected by Janeczko calls into question binaries of word and image and reminds us, as did the Dadaists and, more emphatically, the Lettrisme movement, that words themselves are images, are material, that they matter, that they *are* matter, and that through these poetries children can learn new ways of reading, new ways of relating to texts, new ways of constructing and writing about their world.

Children's poetry as a genre is surprisingly accepting of these writerly texts. As we will see in the coda to this book, concrete and visual poetry find a home much more readily in mainstream anthologies for children than in mainstream anthologies for adults. Highlighting the problematics of representation, naming, and signification, these playful poems help to encourage children (and adults) to become resisting readers, oppositional readers, skeptical readers, productive readers. Closer attention to visual poetry for children will reveal these texts as writerly ones that, in the words of Roland Barthes, "make the reader no longer a consumer, but a producer of texts" (4).

Coda

Toward a Canon of U.S. Children's Poetry

> Cannon to right of them,
> Cannon to left of them,
> Cannon in front of them[.]

Alfred, Lord Tennyson, "The Charge of the Light Brigade"

> [. . .] and what a pretty rose of fire bloomed
> over Cranrobert's hill, though it smelled of bone:
> splinters of oaken cannon & horsen leg
> shot into the nearer air[.]

Gabriel Gudding, "Charge of the L. B."

The primary purpose of this book has been to sketch a working map of the terrain of contemporary American children's poetry and to continue the work begun in Morag Styles's 1998 study, *From the Garden to the Street,* the first extended, general study of English-language children's poetry. Styles's text is, as Anita Tarr writes in her review, "a masterly piece of scholarship," one that will undoubtedly "function as a guidepost for other works to follow" ("Still" 195). Tarr concludes her review with a quotation from *Garden,* urging others to continue the work begun by Styles, to extend the parameters of discourse surrounding children's poetry. Styles writes, "The challenges are endless and there is still so much work to be done in this field. I hope others will take up the challenge and carry on the scholarship in this deeply fascinating area of study. If this book helps anyone to embark on that journey, I will be satisfied" (xxviii). As excellent as *From the Garden to the Street* is, it was met with much negative criticism, primarily for its lack of balance, as it focuses largely on British verse, relegating contemporary American children's poetry to a short, two-page section in the last chapter. (In an e-mail correspondence, Styles mentioned to me her desire to produce a second work concentrating on the history of poetry in the United States.)

Less positive than Tarr, Neil Philip writes, "*From the Garden to the Street* is, I'm sorry to say, absolutely hopeless on the American tradition" (10). Philip is correct, but Styles is not alone in her neglect of U.S. children's poetry, and given that she is from Great Britain, it is not surprising that she would begin her analysis of children's poetry close to home. The first sustained and substantial general treatment of children's poetry (outside of genre studies concentrating on, for instance, nonsense verse), *Garden* follows the trends set by the majority of journal articles on the subject of children's poetry, closely and sensitively exploring the rich British and Canadian traditions to the neglect of the poetry produced in the United States.

Garden has been greeted with criticism because of the gaps in the text, gaps that are necessary and not surprising given its scope and its length. Her book is subtitled "Three Hundred Years of Poetry for Children," a tall order for a text weighing in at a little over three hundred pages. Though my ambitions for this study are more modest than Styles's, limiting my focus to the last forty or so years, I can understand the inevitability of the gaps found in *Garden,* for even with my book's more limited scope, its gaps are manifest. My aims are threefold: to suggest the complexities of contemporary poetry for children written in the United States, to situate the competing traditions of U.S. children's poetry in their larger social and poetic contexts, and to propose several avenues for continued research. This coda, then, is less a conclusion than an acceptance of Tarr's challenge "to journey onward" by offering several suggestions for where we might travel ("Still" 200). One of these avenues concerns canon and canon formation. There are competing canons in U.S. children's poetry, a set of favorites found in each of the four modes discussed in this book: playground poetry, official school poetry, domesticated playground poetry, and visual poetry. As chapter 1 shows, Robert Frost is a central figure in the canon of official school poetry, just as the many variants of "Joy to the World" and "Ms. Lucy" occupy a privileged space in the oral tradition of playground poetry. Literary canons are slippery things, but they have been written, even as they are constantly revised, interrogated, and revised again. As of yet, a canon of U.S. children's poetry has remained unwritten, and no study has been undertaken exploring how the canon implied by children's anthologies might have been formed.

Alan Golding writes, "In the last decade's widespread critical and theoretical grappling with questions of canonicity, little sustained attention has been paid specifically to canon formation in American poetry" (xiii). This claim holds doubly true for American children's poetry. Even books—like Golding's—that do seek to discuss the canon of contemporary American poetry ignore completely the place of children's poetry in these canons, ignoring even the children's poetry produced by canonical adult poets. Jed Rasula's *American Poetry Wax Museum* similarly forgets children's poetry, even as it discusses Kenneth Koch, Donald Hall, X. J. Kennedy, Louis Untermeyer, and other major figures who study, write, and anthologize poetry for the young. In his otherwise notable *Cold War Poetry*, Edward Brunner recovers and discusses neglected female poets, spending significant time on the value of the domestic space in '50s verse and the emphasis poetic culture placed on pedagogy, all the while forgetting children's poetry completely. For a scholar who intends to reexamine a time in terms of that which is overwritten and forgotten, this seems a surprising bout of amnesia, especially considering that he includes an entire chapter on Richard Wilbur—who has written fine children's poetry—and carefully discusses John Ciardi's preoccupation with education. In *American Poetry Wax Museum* Rasula coins the word *canontology,* a hybrid of *canon* and *ontology,* "to signify the criteria for existence—the modes of being and of appearance—that are stipulated by canonical issues" (471). No doubt, then, if "Canontology has to do with sanctioned prescriptions for being, which translates in a given generic setting to *styles of belonging*" (471; italics in the original), then children's poetry is a mode of being that most of the academy deems beneath its notice, or, more accurately, children's poetry is a mode of being that is simply *not noticed.* It does not belong in studies of adult poetry, just as most studies of children's poetry often turn a blind eye to the adult poetic traditions. Children's poetry, especially in the United States, operates in a sphere apart from "real" poetry, these two worlds divided by a stark line drawn by both critics and poets—Theodore Roethke being one of the few canonical poets who actively strove to blur it. Perhaps the one place these lines are consistently blurred is in poetry anthologies for the young, where one might find Shel Silverstein in the same collection as Gertrude Stein.

Chapter 1 broached the subject of canon formation in U.S. children's poetry, tracing Robert Frost's emergence as the official school poet of the United States. But before we can embark on a systematic study of canon formation in U.S. children's poetry, we must first suggest what that canon might be. The shelves at most U.S. bookstores insist that Shel Silverstein, Jack Prelutsky, and Dr. Seuss are at the center of the canon, whereas a survey of education textbooks, journal articles, and major U.S. anthologies of children's poetry suggests another canon, one decidedly rooted in the official school poetry paradigm, though domesticated playground poetry certainly has a presence. In his discussion of children's literature "touchstones," Perry Nodelman argues, "An important part of the study of literature is the attempt to understand the difference between good books and mediocre ones, between good books and great ones" ("Introduction" 1). In his introduction to volume 2 of Nodelman's *Touchstones* series (subtitled: *Reflections on the Best in Children's Literature*), Malcolm Usrey asserts, "All literature is not created equal" (v). He continues, arguing, "Some [literature] is better, and the essays in this book seek to show why and how some myths, legends, folk tales and poetry are better, why and how some works of literature are deemed touchstones" (v).

Undoubtedly we all create hierarchies of value, preferring, in some contexts, one poem or collection over another. But the canon described in this coda is based on a close examination of eight major anthologies of children's poetry, all edited by Americans. I leave the judgment of criteria to other studies. My discussion of this canon is informed by John Timberman Newcomb's focus on the "historical grounds" of canonicity, a focus shaped by "the theoretical principle of the contingency of value in specific instances of cultural activities" (4, 6). Different texts have different values for different people at different historical moments. The shift from the lighthearted, mid-century nature lyric in the late '50s and early '60s was not a symptom of a broad cultural enlightenment, but rather a complex manifestation of the changing tastes of reviewers, anthologists, publishers, and poets. McCord's collected poems, *One at a Time,* which exemplifies dominant, mid-century trends in U.S. children's poetry, was selected by the Children's Literature Association as a "touchstone," one of only three titles written by U.S. children's poets on the list.[1] That so few titles by U.S. children's poets were selected by the Children's Literature Association Canon Committee (the group who determined the "touchstones" list) emphasizes the lack of critical attention paid to U.S. children's poetry. As Nodelman writes, the Canon Committee was looking not only for works that "combined distinctiveness with popularity" but also works that "elicited [. . .] discussion"—that is, works that "were frequently the subjects of papers at conferences and articles in journals" ("Introduction" 7). As we have seen, U.S. children's poetry, while certainly distinctive and sometimes popular, has not been the subject of much discussion.

Golding's call for a synthesis of the two competing theories of canonicity—the aesthetic ("the view that writers make the canon") and the institutional ("the view that critics, teachers, and the academy do so")—seems appropriate when discussing the canon of U.S. children's poetry (xv). The editors of the most prestigious and popular children's anthologies, including the eight I have selected, are generally either poets or critics, sometimes both, and their choices of the adult poetry to include in their children's anthologies neatly align with the critical assessment of poetic value. Canonical U.S. poets like Robert Frost, Theodore Roethke, and Carl Sandburg are represented in all the anthologies selected, and Emily Dickinson, Langston Hughes, Walt Whitman, and William Carlos Williams are found in nearly all. It is plain that the editors' aesthetic values emerge not so much from the canonical selections—Frost, again, appears in all of the selected anthologies—but from the poets who were chosen to fill the spaces between these heavy-hitters. Nevertheless, I have tried to choose anthologies with editors from differing ideological standpoints and from a variety of historical moments. Furthermore, I chose comprehensive anthologies, hoping that they will provide a clearer picture of the major children's poets (and the major children's poems) in the United States.

Again, this canon is descriptive, not prescriptive, formulated as groundwork for future inquiry rather than foreclosing it. The eight anthologies I have selected are, in order of publication:

1. Louis Untermeyer's *The Golden Treasury of Poetry* (1959)

2. Stephen Dunning, Edward Lueders, and Hugh Smith's *Reflections on a Gift of Watermelon Pickle . . . and Other Modern Verse* (1966)

3. X. J. and Dorothy Kennedy's *Knock at a Star: A Child's Introduction to Poetry* (1982)

4. Jack Prelutsky's *The Random House Book of Poetry for Children* (1983)

5. Kenneth Koch's *Talking to the Sun: An Illustrated Anthology of Poems for Young People* (1985)

6. Elizabeth Hauge Sword and Victoria McCarthy's *A Child's Anthology of Poetry* (1995)

7. X. J. and Dorothy Kennedy's *Knock at a Star: A Child's Introduction to Poetry* (1999, rev. ed.)

8. Donald Hall's *The Oxford Illustrated Book of American Children's Poems* (1999).

At the time of this writing, all of these anthologies are still in print (save the first edition of *Knock at a Star*), and are all readily available at most bookstores.[2] This fact alone makes them notable, especially Louis Untermeyer's text, which has been in print since 1959. In *Children's Literature in the Elementary School*, Charlotte S. Huck, Susan Helper, and Janet Hickman note, "Today poetry anthologies do not stay in print as long as they used to because time limits are usually placed on permissions to use certain poems. This has meant the publication of fewer large anthologies and the proliferation of many specialized collections containing fewer than twenty poems" (481).[3] I stayed away from anthologies with few poems—Donald Hall's *The Oxford Illustrated Book of American Children's Poems* is the shortest, with only seventy-six poems—and have avoided thematic anthologies, like Harold Bloom and Donald Hall's *The Wind and the Rain* (1961), Myra Cohn Livingston's excellent *Why Am I Grown So Cold? Poems of the Unknowable* (1982), or Lee Bennett Hopkins's *My America: A Poetry Atlas of the United States* (2000). Nevertheless, most of the thematic anthologies that I have encountered generally follow selection trends that are similar to those of the comprehensive anthologies. Many of the same authors are to be found, though the individual poems change. Sometimes, however, a theme is so specialized that it is impossible to choose from the canon. The theme of Paul B. Janeczko's *A Poke in the I: A Collection of Concrete Poems* (2001), for instance, precludes the inclusion of all the most common poets, save, perhaps, E. E. Cummings. However, *Why Am I Grown So Cold?*, which has the less restrictive theme of "the unknowable," includes, among other familiar poets, Emily Dickinson (three poems), Robert Frost (three poems), Theodore Roethke (one poem), and Carl Sandburg (one poem). *My America* includes work by Langston Hughes, David McCord, Lilian Moore, and Carl Sandburg. These poets are central to the canon of official school poetry, their poems appearing in most anthologies featuring a sizable number of U.S. poets, regardless of their editor's ideological bent.[4]

Untermeyer's Golden Book anthology undoubtedly is influenced by the great British anthologies that preceded it. Like Walter de la Mare's now out-of-print *Come Hither* (1923), *The Golden Treasury* includes adult British poets John Clare (four poems), William Cowper (two poems), Thomas Hood (three poems), Alexander Pope (two poems), Alfred Tennyson (five poems), and William Wordsworth (seven poems). In addition to Wordsworth, Untermeyer also includes all of the major British romantics, William Blake (eight poems), Lord George Gordon Byron (one poem), Samuel Taylor Coleridge (three poems), John Keats (six poems), and Percy Bysshe Shelley (two poems). Already the brightest stars of the British children's literature canon—Lewis Carroll (six poems), Edward Lear (seven poems), de la Mare (three poems), Christina Rossetti (six poems), and Robert Louis Stevenson (ten poems)—are all represented. But regardless of the large British presence in his anthology, Untermeyer's selection of U.S. poets proves prescient: of the ten U.S. poets who appear in six or more of the eight selected anthologies, only two do not appear in Untermeyer's: Langston Hughes and William Carlos Williams.[5] Given Untermeyer's aesthetic leanings, Williams's exclusion is not surprising, and not a single African American poet is to be found in the anthology.

Stephen Dunning, Edward Lueders, and Hugh Smith's exceptional *Reflections on a Gift of Watermelon Pickle . . .* strives to acquaint young readers with modern poetry, much in the same way John Ciardi sought to introduce the "general reader" to mid-century poetry with his *Mid-Century American Poetry* (1950). The book begins with a note that includes "four ideas that will help you read" the poems (14), ideas in the spirit of the thirteen "principles" for reading poetry that Ciardi laid out in the introduction to his own poetry in *Mid-Century*.[6] Unlike Untermeyer, who intersperses the poems with commentary, the editors of *Reflections* save their commentary until the end, in a section called "Interpretation." This anthology is obviously intended to appeal to both teachers and children and in this respect anticipates the Kennedys' *Knock at a Star.* No doubt this pedagogical bent—along with the quality verse it contains—played a part in its place in the Children's Literature Association's "touchstones" list. The authors of *Children's Literature in the Elementary School* call *Reflections* "One of the most exciting current anthologies" (485), a remarkable statement, considering that the anthology was almost thirty years old in 1993, when the fifth edition was published. *Children's Literature in the Elementary School* was first published, however, in 1968, two years after *Reflections.* Even though this bit of text survives from that earlier edition, the editors left it unchanged for good reason. Though the layout is somewhat dated, the poems seem contemporary enough, especially when compared to the selections in Untermeyer's collection.

The pedagogical thrust of *Knock at a Star* is similar to that of *Reflections.* A collection marked by poetic diversity, *Knock at a Star* includes poetry written expressly for children, as well as poetry written for adults that might appeal to children. Like Donald Hall, X. J. Kennedy's genealogy can be traced back to Untermeyer (who was close friends with Robert Frost) and the academic traditions of the late '50s and early '60s. Considering their aesthetic roots, the Kennedys make some striking choices. They include, for instance, concrete/visual poet Ian Hamilton Finley's poetry (work intended for adults) in their *Knock at a Star,* while X. J. Kennedy and New Formalist Dana Gioia elect to leave Finley out of their adult anthology *An Introduction to Poetry.* The Kennedys also include "Concrete Cat,"[7] Myra Cohn Livingston's found/concrete poem "Four Way Stop," Gertrude Stein's "I Am Rose," poems from Objectivist Charles Reznikoff, the New York School's Kenneth Koch, Carl Sandburg, and many other intriguing choices. In his anthology of Dada poetry, *Dada Market,* Willard Bohn reminds us that the Dadaists—and, I might add, most experimental poetries—are often dismissed for their radical defamiliarization, for their resistance to conventional notions of "critical analysis" and reading practices (xv). He continues, noting that Dada in particular is equated with "infantile behavior" (xv). It is uncertain, then, whether the Kennedys are willfully challenging the canon, or, rather, if they are putting poems they believe are "infantile" in their children's anthology. Unlike Dunning and company, the Kennedys do not shy away from domesticated playground poetry, selecting poems by both Shel Silverstein and Jack Prelutsky. If X. J. Kennedy's compelling essay "Strict and Loose Nonsense: Two Worlds of Children's Verse" is any indication, their decision to include domesticated playground poetry was not merely acquiescence to popular taste, for in it Kennedy speaks highly of both Silverstein's and Prelutsky's poetry. In this essay Kennedy notes that Silverstein might appear in more anthologies had he not insisted "that anyone who reprints one of his poems must reprint the illustration too" (230).

Kenneth Koch's *Talking to the Sun* is similar to the Kennedys' anthology in that he too includes quite a number of surprising choices, though Koch's choices, unlike the Kennedys', align more obviously with his aesthetic sensibility. Kenneth Koch's career is famous for canon challenging, but regardless of his or the Kennedys' motivations, the poetic variety in both of these collections is a useful starting place for teachers and children to question the dominant conception of poetry and poetic value. Though the selections in Koch's anthology are more idiosyncratic than most (save, perhaps, *Reflections*), Koch nonetheless includes ten of the thirteen poets who appear in six or more anthologies, omitting only Elizabeth Coatsworth, Eve Merriam, and William Jay Smith. Given that New York School poetry is often noted for its surrealistic impulses, we should not be surprised when noted Dadaist/surrealist André Breton appears in *Talking to the Sun*. Koch's anthology also includes the visual poem "Heart Crown and Mirror," by symbolist and Dadaist precursor Guillaume Apollinaire, as well as selections from Gertrude Stein's *Tender Buttons*. *Talking to the Sun* is notable both for its inclusion of a wide array of poets and poetries and for Koch's conscious dismantling of the often problematic genre distinction between children's poetry and adult poetry. Furthermore, Koch juxtaposes visual art with poetry, creating a rich and heterogeneous anthology. However, Koch finds little room for poetry written especially for children, whether by U.S. or British authors, nor does he include poems written *by* children, despite his claims in *Rose, Where Did You Get That Red?* that such poetry is quality poetry.

The Random House Book of Poetry conspicuously differs from the others, as it eschews instruction and places "the accent [. . .] on humor and light verse" (19). Complaining that "something happens to [young people's] early love affair with poetry," Prelutsky hopes to remedy this estrangement with a rousing collection of comic poetry (18). Though Prelutsky does include "many poignant and serious poems," he praises the "easygoing pleasure" offered by the majority, avoiding poetry he thinks children may find "boring and irrelevant, too difficult or too dull" (18). If the other anthologies emphasize official school poetry, Prelutsky's anthology accentuates domesticated playground poetry. On the other hand, Donald Hall's anthology, a condensed version of his more scholarly endeavor, *The Oxford Book of Children's Verse in America* (1985), downplays playground poetry of any variety and certainly contains less stylistic diversity, though it is one of only two anthologies that include Dr. Seuss. Prelutsky's is the other, with two pieces by Seuss. Hall's anthology, like *Reflections* and *Knock at a Star,* suggests a pedagogical subtext, even though it is intended, more so than *The Oxford Book of Children's Verse,* for a child audience. Hall's short preface contains vestigial elements of its longer predecessor, briefly outlining a history of children's poetry in America, and ending with the patriotic thought, "With an old picture beside it, a poem may also preserve a moment of the American past" (7).

Finally, Sword and McCarthy's *A Child's Anthology of Poetry* attempts to gather poetry that will introduce "a young reader to the excitement, the beauty, the power, and the fun of poetry" (xv). The poems included were recommended by a thirteen-member advisory board, comprised of well-known and largely mainstream poets, Louise Glück, Jorie Graham, Edward Hirsch, and Mark Strand among them. This notable body of advisers (which includes no children's poets that I recognize) distinguishes *A Child's Anthology*, but the poems included are nonetheless very similar to those in other anthologies. Of all the poets who appear in five or more anthologies (twenty-eight poets), only five do not appear in *A Child's Anthology*: William Jay Smith, John Ciardi, Oliver Herford, David McCord, and Phyllis McGinley. Curiously, all five of these poets, save two—Ciardi and Smith—are principally known for their children's poetry or light verse (in the case of Herford), and most, incidentally, are omitted by Koch, whose anthology features even fewer poems by children's poets.[8] The canon suggested by this and the other seven anthologies is one marked by a preponderance of well-represented writers of adult work. Why U.S. children's anthologies, as opposed to English and Canadian, turn to adult poets much to the neglect of children's poets should be a question pursued in future investigations into U.S. canon formation.

As the preceding discussion suggests, the poets who appear in all eight selected anthologies—and, in fact, most comprehensive anthologies of children's poetry, whether British or U.S.—are not surprising: E. E. Cummings, Robert Frost, Theodore Roethke, and Carl Sandburg. Again, none of these four writes primarily for children. Though five of the nine poets who appear in six to seven anthologies write primarily for children, three of those five are British poets: Lewis Carroll, Walter de la Mare, and Edward Lear. Of the U.S. poets in six to seven anthologies, only two are children's poets (Elizabeth Coatsworth and Eve Merriam), the other four being known chiefly for their adult poetry (Emily Dickinson, Langston Hughes, William Jay Smith, and William Carlos Williams). Add to this six E. E. Cummings, Robert Frost, Theodore Roethke, and Carl Sandburg, and we have the core of the U.S. children's poetry canon. A majority of these ten central poets are found and well represented in just about any comprehensive children's poetry anthology with a substantial U.S. presence. The reason why Carroll, de la Mare, and Edward Lear—certainly among the best-known children's poets in the English language—appear in only six of the eight is that they do not meet the selection criteria for either *Reflections*, an anthology of modern poetry, or Hall's collection, which features exclusively U.S. poets. Surprisingly, A. A. Milne, another well-known and often discussed British poet, appears in only two anthologies: Untermeyer's already heavily British volume *The Golden Treasury* and Prelutsky's *The Random House Book of Poetry*. Prelutsky includes Milne's "The More It Snows," and Untermeyer includes "The Four Friends." Curiously, all of the British poets found in the list of thirteen write primarily for children, whereas only two of the U.S. poets do. The core of U.S. children's poetry is of the official school variety, mostly lighter poetry concerning weather, seasons, or animals. Emily Dickinson is the most well-represented U.S. poet, appearing twenty-eight times, and represented by twenty-two poems. The second most well-represented U.S. poet is Coatsworth, with fifteen poems. Roethke and Smith manage thirteen, whereas Hughes and Frost are represented by twelve.[9]

Rasula writes, "Even the most homogeneous anthologies will *appear* to initiates and insiders to capture some variety" (464). He continues, noting that it is rare to encounter an anthology that "attempt[s] to conceive heterogeneity from outside their own partisan coordinates" (465). The same holds true for the anthologies surveyed here. Prelutsky, in his attempt to capture "the easygoing pleasure" of poetry, places "the accent [. . .] on humor and light verse" (18, 19), whereas Sword and McCarthy, in their pursuit of "fine poetry within the grasp of an elementary student" (xv), feature more highbrow fare. Nevertheless, though there is the appearance of variety, these anthologies—all of the eight, in fact—achieve a remarkable sameness. This sameness is startling when one considers the sheer numbers of poets writing for children in the United States today. Though Mother Goose is often represented in children's poetry collections, only the Kennedys' anthology features playground poetry, and no poetry by child poets is to be found. Furthermore, even the sampling of adult poets is surprisingly one-dimensional, all of the most common poets falling neatly in the voice-lyric paradigm. Very few experimental or avant-garde poets find their way into these anthologies. And even looking past the issue of stylistic diversity, the number of white male poets is strikingly large. Of the seventy-two U.S. poets who appear at least three times in any one of the selected anthologies, only thirty-one are women. Nine of the top twenty-seven most well-represented U.S. poets are women, and among these twenty-seven Gwendolyn Brooks and Langston Hughes are the only nonwhite poets. The implications of these findings deserve to be addressed.

It seems the stronger anthology for children would be one in which various and sometimes incommensurate poetries exist in dialogue with one another. This arrangement would allow a child—a beginning reader—to start her reading experiences with as heterogeneous a conception of poetry as possible. A heterogeneous collection of poetry would allow for new, progressive understandings of the world, new reading strategies, new ways of thinking. This juxtaposition of competing aesthetics could encourage multiple strategies for meaning-making without hierarchy, foregrounding difference. Of all the anthologists surveyed, *Knock at a Star* and *Talking to the Sun* make the best attempt at such a heterogeneous anthology. Such anthologies—more than, say, *A Child's Anthology*—provide occasions for young readers to question matters of taste and the ideological assumptions underlying taste. Making available to children a wider diversity of poetry allows them the opportunity to question canons and build their own ideas of poetic merit. For experienced readers, visual and nonsense poetry critique traditional ways of making meaning. For beginning readers, visual poetry and nonsense can provide a different starting point, a different base.

In *When You've Made It Your Own . . . Teaching Poetry to Young People*, Gregory Denman stresses "THERE IS MORE TO POETRY THAN SHEL SILVERSTEIN" (83). He continues, "[Y]ou no more need to teach children the poetry of Shel Silverstein than to give them lessons in eating McDonald's hamburgers, fries, and a shake" (83). This sort of condescension is profoundly dismissive and is perhaps the root reason why more playground poetry—domesticated or otherwise—is not found commonly in children's anthologies; and it is certainly the reason why such poetry is not found in anthologies for adults. Denman and other critics who dismiss playground and other seemingly simple poetries do so by, in the words of Beverly Clark, "Rely[ing] on New Critical strategies for criticizing a work, strategies that privilege complexity, so that it will be difficult to find anything to say about seemingly 'simple' works of literature" (240–41). These same reading strategies are used to dismiss Dadaist, surrealist, and concrete poetry. I suggest that there is more to children's poetry than the official school mode, more to poetry than the poetries championed by New Critics. If poetry is to remain a rich, vibrant, and relevant art form, it is important for scholars, teachers, publishers, and anthologists to acknowledge counter-canon poetries; to place radical poetries next to conservative ones, children's poetry next to adult, and school poetry next to playground poetry; to willingly expose children to the diversity of expression poetry offers; and to affirm the poetry they already know.

Appendix A
Most Commonly Anthologized Poets

Below is a list of the poets who appear three or more times in any one of the following eight anthologies:

(A) Louis Untermeyer, *The Golden Treasury of Poetry* (1959)

(B) Stephen Dunning, Edward Lueders, and Hugh Smith, *Reflections on a Gift of Watermelon Pickle . . . and Other Modern Verse* (1966)

(C) X. J. and Dorothy Kennedy, *Knock at a Star A Child's Introduction to Poetry* (1982)

(D) Jack Prelutsky, *The Random House Book of Poetry for Children* (1983)

(E) Kenneth Koch, *Talking to the Sun: An Illustrated Anthology of Poems for Young People* (1985)

(F) Elizabeth Hauge Sword and Victoria McCarthy, *A Child's Anthology of Poetry* (1995)

(G) X. J. and Dorothy Kennedy, *Knock at a Star: A Child's Introduction to Poetry* (rev. ed., 1999)

(H) Donald Hall, *The Oxford Illustrated Book of American Children's Poems* (1999).

Poets	Number of Appearances in Each Anthology (A–H)								
	A	B	C	D	E	F	G	H	
Poets in eight anthologies									
Cummings, E. E.	1	1	1	2	2	3	1	1	8
Frost, Robert	2	1	2	3	2	4	1	1	8
Roethke, Theodore	1	2	3	5	1	6	1	2	8
Sandburg, Carl	2	2	1	3	1	2	1	2	8

Poets in seven anthologies

Coatsworth, Elizabeth	5	2	1	5	0	1	2	2	7
Dickinson, Emily	10	0	1	2	4	8	1	2	7
Hughes, Langston	0	2	2	4	2	2	3	3	7

Poets in six anthologies

Carroll, Lewis	6	*	2	5	3	4	2	*	6[a]
De la Mare, Walter	3	1	0	5	1	2	1	*	6
Lear, Edward	7	*	3	3	1	1	1	*	6
Merriam, Eve	0	3	4	5	0	1	5	1	6
Smith, William Jay	3	2	3	6	0	0	1	1	6
Williams, William Carlos	0	3	2	1	5	4	1	0	6

Poets in five anthologies

Blake, William	8	*	1	2	3	5	0	*	5
Brooks, Gwendolyn	0	0	1	2	0	1	2	1	5
Ciardi, John	0	2	1	5	0	0	2	1	5
Field, Rachel	0	0	1	6	0	5	1	1	5
Frances, Robert	0	3	1	1	0	1	1	0	5
Herford, Oliver	1	1	1	3	0	0	1	0	5
Kennedy, X. J.	0	0	2	4	0	1	2	1	5[b]
McCord, David	2	1	2	5	0	0	2	1	5
McGinley, Phyllis	0	1	1	3	0	0	1	1	5
Millay, Edna St. Vincent	0	1	0	1	2	3	0	1	5
Nash, Ogden	3	0	3	7	0	3	2	0	5
Rossetti, Christina	6	*	0	6	1	5	1	*	5
Stevenson, Robert Louis	10	*	1	3	0	5	1	*	5
Tennyson, Lord Alfred	5	*	0	1	2	5	1	*	5
Whitman, Walt	3	*	1	0	1	2	1	0	5

Poets in four anthologies

Field, Eugene	3	0	0	1	0	2	0	1	4
Guiterman, Arthur	0	2	1	4	0	0	0	1	4

Housman, A. E.	0	0	1	1	1	3	0	*		4
Kuskin, Karla	0	0	1	6	0	0	1	1		4
Lawrence, D. H.	0	0	1	0	5	1	1	*		4
Longfellow, Henry W.	7	*	0	1	0	4	0	1		4
Prelutsky, Jack	0	0	0	28	0	2	2	1		4
Roberts, Elizabeth Madox	3	0	1	2	0	0	0	1		4
Silverstein, Shel	0	0	1	7	0	1	0	1		4
Yeats, William Butler	0	0	1	1	3	5	0	*		4

Poets in three anthologies

Bishop, Elizabeth	1	0	0	0	1	3	0	0		3
Clare, John	4	0	0	0	1	1	0	0		3
Emerson, Ralph Waldo	3	0	0	1	0	0	0	1		3
Farjeon, Eleanor	2	0	0	7	0	1	0	0		3
Fisher, Aileen	0	0	1	4	0	0	1	0		3
Herrick, Robert	2	0	1	0	3	0	0	0		3
Hoberman, Mary Ann	0	0	0	7	0	0	2	1		3
Jarrell, Randall	0	0	1	1	0	1	0	0		3
Keats, John	6	*	0	0	1	2	0	0		3
Lee, Dennis	0	0	1	5	0	0	2	*		3
Livingston, Myra Cohn	0	0	3	4	0	0	3	0		3
Moore, Lilian	0	0	1	7	0	0	1	0		3
Morrison, Lillian	0	0	3	5	0	0	1	0		3
O'Neill, Mary	0	0	1	5	0	0	1	0		3
Shakespeare, William	4	*	0	1	4	0	0	*		3
Shelley, Percy Bysshe	2	*	0	0	3	1	0	*		3
Stevens, Wallace	0	0	0	0	3	2	1	0		3
Wordsworth, William	7	*	0	0	1	5	0	*		3

Poets in two anthologies

Aldis, Dorothy	0	0	0	5	0	1	0	0		2
Aldrich, Thomas Bailey	3	*	0	1	0	0	0	0		2
Bodecker, N. M.	0	0	0	4	0	0	3	*		2
Buson, Yosa	0	*	0	0	1	3	0	*		2
Cole, William	0	0	1	3	0	0	0	0		2
Frost, Frances	0	3	0	3	0	0	0	0		2

Hall, Donald	0	3	1	0	0	0	0	0		2
Hardy, Thomas	0	0	0	0	2	4	0	0		2
Holman, Felice	0	0	0	5	0	0	2	0		2
Hubbell, Patricia	0	0	0	3	0	0	1	0		2
Issa, Kobayashi	0	0	0	0	2	7	0	0		2
Katz, Bobbi	0	0	0	5	0	0	1	0		2
Kinnell, Galway	0	0	1	0	0	3	0	0		2
Kooser, Ted	0	0	3	0	0	0	4	0		2
Monro, Harold	3	1	0	0	0	0	0	0		2
Reeves, James	2	0	0	4	0	0	0	0		2
Starbird, Kaye	0	0	1	4	0	0	0	0		2
Turner, Nancy Byrd	0	0	0	3	0	1	0	0		2
Viorst, Judith	0	0	0	3	0	0	2	0		2
Zolotow, Charlotte	0	0	0	3	0	0	1	0		2

Poets in one anthology

Asch, Frank	0	0	0	4	0	0	0	0		1
Bell, J. J. (John Joy)	0	0	0	3	0	0	0	0		1
Brooks, Walter R.	0	0	0	4	0	0	0	0		1
Browning, Robert	4	*	0	0	0	0	0	*		1
De Andrade, Carlos D.	0	0	0	0	0	3	0	0		1
Eluard, Paul	0	0	0	0	3	0	0	0		1
Fraser, Kathleen	0	0	0	3	0	0	0	0		1
Hoban, Russell	0	0	0	5	0	0	0	0		1
Hood, Thomas	3	0	0	0	0	0	0	0		1
Jacobs, Leland B.	0	0	0	3	0	0	0	0		1
Lewis, J. Patrick	0	0	0	0	0	0	3	0		1
Lewis, Michael	3	0	0	0	0	0	0	0		1
Lorca, Federico Garcia	0	0	0	0	3	0	0	*		1
Lowell, James Russell	3	0	0	0	0	0	0	0		1
Miller, Mary Britton	0	0	0	4	0	0	0	0		1
Milligan, Spike	0	0	0	3	0	0	0	0		1
O'Hara, Frank	0	0	0	0	5	0	0	0		1
Payne, Nina	0	0	0	3	0	0	0	0		1
Poe, Edgar Allan	0	*	0	0	0	4	0	0		1
Ridlon, Marci	0	0	0	4	0	0	0	0		1
Rieu, E. V.	0	0	0	6	0	0	0	0		1

Rilke, Rainer Maria	0	0	0	0	3	0	0	*	1
Rimbaud, Arthur	0	0	0	0	3	0	0	*	1
Schuyler, James	0	0	0	0	3	0	0	0	1
Simic, Charles	0	0	0	0	0	4	0	0	1
Spilka, Arnold	0	0	0	5	0	0	0	0	1
Thackeray, William M.	3	0	0	0	0	0	0	0	1
Thompson, Dorothy Brown	0	0	0	3	0	0	0	0	1
Untermeyer, Louis	12	0	0	0	0	0	0	0	1[c]
Yolen, Jane	0	0	0	3	0	0	0	0	1

a. An asterisk denotes a poet's absence because he or she does not fit the editor's selection rubric (Hall printed only U.S. poets; Dunning et al. selected only modern poets).

b. Both of Kennedy's poems in C and G are credited to Dorthi Charles, a pseudonym.

c. Three of Untermeyer's poems found in *The Golden Treasury* are attributed to Michael Lewis, a pseudonym.

Appendix B
Most Commonly Anthologized Poets Grouped by Nationality

Please refer to appendix A for anthology titles and authors.

I. U.S. poets with three or more poems in at least one anthology (A–H)

Poet	Period[a]
Aldis, Dorothy	20th century
Aldrich, Thomas Bailey	1836–1907 (pre-20th century)
Asch, Frank	20th century
Bodecker, Niels Mogans	20th century (born in Copenhagen, Denmark)
Bishop, Elizabeth	20th century
Brooks, Gwendolyn	20th century
Brooks, Walter R.	1886–1958 (20th century)
Ciardi, John	20th century
Coatsworth, Elizabeth	20th century
Cole, William	20th century
Cummings, E. E.	20th century
Dickinson, Emily	pre-20th century
Emerson, Ralph Waldo	pre-20th century
Field, Eugene	pre-20th century
Field, Rachel	20th century
Fisher, Aileen	20th century
Francis, Robert	20th century
Fraser, Kathleen	20th century
Frost, Frances	20th century
Frost, Robert	20th century
Guiterman, Arthur	1871–1943 (20th century)
Hall, Donald	20th century
Herford, Oliver	1863–1935 (20th century)
Hoban, Russell	20th century

Hoberman, Mary Ann	20th century
Holman, Felice	20th century
Hubbell, Patricia	20th century
Hughes, Langston	20th century
Jacobs, Leland B.	20th century
Jarrell, Randall	20th century
Katz, Bobbi	20th century
Kennedy, X. J. (D. Charles)	20th century
Kinnell, Galway	20th century
Kooser, Ted	20th century
Kuskin, Karla	20th century
Lewis, J. Patrick	20th century
Livingston, Myra Cohn	20th century
Longfellow, Henry W.	pre-20th century
Lowell, James Russell	pre-20th century
McCord, David	20th century
McGinley, Phyllis	20th century
Merriam, Eve	20th century
Millay, Edna St. Vincent	20th century
Miller, Mary Britton	1883–1975 (20th century)
Moore, Lilian	20th century
Morrison, Lillian	20th century
Nash, Ogden	20th century
O'Hara, Frank	20th century
O'Neill, Mary	20th century
Payne, Nina	20th century
Poe, Edgar Allan	pre-20th century
Prelutsky, Jack	20th century
Ridlon, Marci[b]	20th century
Roberts, Elizabeth Madox	1842–1913 (20th century)
Roethke, Theodore	20th century
Sandburg, Carl	20th century
Schuyler, James	20th century
Silverstein, Shel	20th century
Simic, Charles	20th century
Smith, William Jay	20th century
Spilka, Arnold	20th century
Starbird, Kaye	20th century
Stevens, Wallace	20th century

Thompson, Dorothy Brown	20th century
Turner, Nancy Byrd	20th century
Untermeyer, Louis	20th century
Viorst, Judith	20th century
Whitman, Walt	pre-20th century
Williams, William Carlos	20th century
Yeats, William Butler	20th century
Yolen, Jane	20th century
Zolotow, Charlotte	20th century

II. British poets with three or more poems in at least one anthology (A–H)

Poet	Approximate Period
Bell, J. J. (John Joy)	1871–1934 (20th century)
Blake, William	pre-20th century
Browning, Robert	pre-20th century
Carroll, Lewis	pre-20th century
Clare, John	pre-20th century
De la Mare, Walter	1873–1956 (20th century)
Farjeon, Eleanor	1881–1965 (20th century)
Hardy, Thomas	pre-20th century
Herrick, Robert	pre-20th century
Hood, Thomas	pre-20th century
Housman, A. E.	1859–1936 (20th century)
Keats, John	pre-20th century
Lawrence, D. H.	20th century
Lear, Edward	pre-20th century
Milligan, Spike	20th century
Reeves, James	20th century
Rieu, E. V.	1887–1972 (20th century)
Rossetti, Christina	pre-20th century
Shakespeare, William	pre-20th century
Shelley, Percy Bysshe	pre-20th century
Stevenson, Robert Louis	pre-20th century
Tennyson, Lord Alfred	pre-20th century
Thackeray, William M.	pre-20th century
Wordsworth, William	pre-20th century

III. Non-British and non-U.S. poets
with three or more poems in at least one anthology (A–H)

Poet	Nationality	Approximate Period
Buson, Yosa	Japan	pre-20th century
De Andrade, Carlos D.	Brazil	20th century
Eluard, Paul	French	1895–1952 (20th century)
Issa, Kobayashi	Japan	pre-20th century
Lee, Dennis	Canada	20th century
Lorca, Federico Garcia	Spain	20th century
Monro, Harold	Belgium	1879–1932 (20th century)
Rilke, Rainer Maria	Germany	1875–1926 (20th century)
Rimbaud, Arthur	France	pre-20th century

a. Because some authors' lives bridge centuries, I have provided dates for those who are either lesser known or especially difficult to categorize because they have, for example, published books in both centuries. With better-known poets, I have followed convention (Carl Sandburg, for instance, while born in 1878, is commonly considered a twentieth-century author, so his dates are not given).

b. Marci Ridlon is a pseudonym for Marcia Ridlon Balterman.

Appendix C

Most Commonly Anthologized U.S. Poets and the Poems Representing Them: A Descriptive Canon

Please refer to appendix A for anthology titles and authors.

I. U.S. poets appearing in eight anthologies

E. E. Cummings
>Total Appearances: 12
>Number of Unique Poems: 6
>
>Poems:
>"anyone lived in a pretty how town"
>"here's a little mouse"
>"hist whist"
>"in Just—"
>"maggie and milly and molly and may"
>"up into the silence the green"

Robert Frost
>Total Appearances: 16
>Number of Unique Poems: 12
>
>Poems:
>"Beyond Words"
>"Canis Major"
>"Dust of Snow"
>"Fireflies in the Garden"
>"Goodbye and Keep Cold"
>"Last Word of a Bluebird as Told to a Child"
>"Mending Wall"
>"The Pasture"

"A Patch of Old Snow"
"The Road Not Taken"
"The Runaway"
"Stopping by Woods on a Snowy Evening"

Theodore Roethke
Total Appearances: 21
Number of Unique Poems: 13

Poems:
"The Bat"
"The Ceiling"
"Child on Top of a Greenhouse"
"Dinky"
"The Lady and the Bear"
"The Lizard"
"The Meadow Mouse"
"Monotony Song"
"My Papa's Waltz"
"Night Journey"
"The Serpent"
"The Sloth"
"The Waking"

Carl Sandburg
Total Appearances: 14
Number of Unique Poems: 7

Poems:
"Arithmetic"
"Buffalo Dusk"
"Fog"
"Lost"
"Splinter"
"We Must Be Polite: (Lessons for Children on How to Behave Under
    Peculiar Circumstances)"
"Yarns" [from *The People, Yes*]

II. U.S. poets appearing in seven anthologies

Elizabeth Coatsworth

Total Appearances: 18
Number of Unique Poems: 15

Poems:
"The Barn"
"The Complete Hen"
"Conquistador"
"Country Barnyard"
"Country Cat"
"March"
"Mountain Brook"
"No Shop Does the Bird Use"
"On a Night of Snow"
"Rhyme"
"Sea Gull"
"Song of the Rabbits Outside the Tavern"
"And Stands There Sighing"
"Swift Things Are Beautiful"
"This Is a Night"

Emily Dickinson

Total Appearances: 28
Number of Unique Poems: 22

Poems:
"Bee! I'm Expecting You"
"A bird came down the walk"
"Certainty"
"A Day"
"The Difference"
"'Hope' is the thing with feathers"
"Hours of Sleep"
"The Hummingbird"
"I met a King this afternoon!"
"I'm Nobody! Who Are You?"

"Indian Summer"
"I never saw a moor"
"The morns are meeker than they were"
"A Narrow Fellow in the Grass"
"Pedigree"
"The Snake"
"The Snow"
"There is no frigate like a book"
"We Like March"
"Who Is the East?"
"The Wind Too up the Northern Things"
"A Word Is Dead"

Langston Hughes
> Total Appearances: 18
> Number of Unique Poems: 12

> Poems:
> "April Rain Song"
> "City"
> "Dreams"
> "Hope"
> "Juke Box Love Song"
> "The Locust Tree in Flower"
> "Miss Blues'es Child"
> "Mother to Son"
> "Oh, God of dust and rainbows"
> "Subway Rush Hour"
> "Too Blue"
> "Winter Moon"

III. U.S. poets appearing in six anthologies

Eve Merriam
> Total Appearances: 19
> Number of Unique Poems: 10

Poems:
"Catch a Little Rhyme"
"Cheers"
"Counting-out Rhyme"
"How to Eat a Poem"
"Landscape"
"Notice to Myself"
"Oz."
"Sing a Song of Subways"
"Two People"
"Windshield Wiper"

William Jay Smith
Total Appearances: 16
Number of Unique Poems: 13

Poems:
"Brooklyn Bridge"
"The Floor and the Ceiling"
"Jittery Jim"
"Lion"
"Love"
"Opossum"
"Said Dorothy Hughes to Helen Hocking"
"Seal"
"[There once was a Young Lady named Rose]"
"[There once was an old lady named Crocket]"
"The Toaster"
"Unicorn"
"Yak"

William Carlos Williams
Total Appearances: 16
Number of Unique Poems: 7

Poems:
"The Great Figure"

"Poem"
"The Red Wheelbarrow"
"Spring and All"
"The Term"
"This is Just to Say"
"To a Poor Old Woman"

Appendix D
Award-Winning Books of Contemporary U.S. Poetry

For the sake of future scholarship, I feature in this appendix a list of award-winning collections of contemporary U.S. children's poetry written by a single author. I have omitted prize-winning poetry anthologies, such as Naomi Shihab Nye's *Is This Forever, or What? Poems & Paintings from Texas* (Greenwillow, 2004), a 2005 Lee Bennett Hopkins Award Honor Book. Also omitted are poetry collections awarded primarily for their illustrations (Caldecott winners, for example) as well as repackaged older poems, such as Bagram Ibatoulline's award-winning *Crossing* (Candlewick, 2001), an illustrated version of a poem from Philip Booth's 1957 collection, *Letter from a Distant Land* (Viking). At the end of this appendix I have also listed the winners of the National Council of Teachers of English Award for Poetry for Children. Established in 1977, this award is not for any individual book of children's poetry but, rather, recognizes an outstanding career in children's poetry.

I. American Library Association (ALA) Notable Children's Books

2005
Grandits, John. *Technically, It's Not My Fault: Concrete Poems* (Clarion)
Grimes, Nikki. *What Is Goodbye?* (Hyperion)
Myers, Walter Dean. *Here in Harlem: Poems in Many Voices* (Holiday House)
Nelson, Marilyn. *Fortune's Bones: The Manumission Requiem* (Front Street)
Prelutsky, Jack. *If Not for the Cat* (Greenwillow)
Scieszka, Jon. *Science Verse* (Viking)

2004
Chandra, Deborah, and Madeleine Comora. *George Washington's Teeth* (Farrar, Straus and Giroux)
Myers, Walter Dean. *Blues Journey* (Holiday House)

2003
Mak, Kam. *My Chinatown: One Year in Poems* (HarperCollins)

Testa, Maria. *Becoming Joe DiMaggio* (Candlewick)

2002
Alarcón, Francisco X. *Iguanas in the Snow* (Children's Book Press)
Creech, Sharon. *Love That Dog* (Joanna Cotler)
Hesse, Karen. *Witness* (Scholastic)
Hoberman, Mary Ann. *You Read to Me, I'll Read to You: Very Short Stories to Read Together* (Megan Tingley)
Nelson, Marilyn. *Carver: A Life in Poems* (Front Street)
Williams, Vera B. *Amber Was Brave, Essie Was Smart* (Greenwillow)

2001
Lewis, J. Patrick. *Freedom Like Sunlight: Praisesongs for Black Americans* (Creative Editions)

2000
George, Kristine O'Connell. *Little Dog Poems* (Clarion)
Smith, Charles R., Jr. *Rimshots: Basketball Pix, Rolls and Rhythms* (Dutton Juvenile)
Stevenson, James. *Candy Corn: Poems* (Greenwillow)
Updike, John. *A Child's Calendar* (Holiday House)

II. Newbery Medal Award

2002 Honor Book
Nelson, Marilyn. *Carver: A Life in Poems* (Front Street)

1998 Medal Winner
Hesse, Karen. *Out of the Dust* (Scholastic)

1989 Medal Winner
Fleischman, Paul. *Joyful Noise: Poems for Two Voices* (Harper)

1982 Medal Winner
Willard, Nancy. *A Visit to William Blake's Inn: Poems for Innocent and Experienced Travelers* (Harcourt)

III. Coretta Scott King Author Awards

2004 Honor Book

Woodson, Jacqueline. *Locomotion* (Putnam Juvenile)

2004: Coretta Scott King/
John Steptoe New Talent Author Award

Smith, Hope Anita. *The Way a Door Closes* (Henry Holt Books for Young Readers)

2003 Winner

Grimes, Nikki. *Bronx Masquerade* (Penguin Putnam Books for Young Readers)

2002 Honor Book

Nelson, Marilyn. *Carver: A Life in Poems* (Front Street)

1999 Honor Books

Grimes, Nikki. *Jazmin's Notebook* (Dial)
Johnson, Angela. *The Other Side: The Shorter Poems* (Orchard)

1984 Winner

Clifton, Lucille. *Everett Anderson's Goodbye* (Henry Holt)

IV. Lee Bennett Hopkins Poetry Award

2005 Winner

Myers, Walter Dean. *Here in Harlem: Poems in Many Voices* (Holiday House)

Honoree

Singer, Marilyn. *Creature Carnival* (Hyperion)

2004 Winner

Mitchell, Stephen. *The Wishing Bone and Other Poems* (Candlewick)

Honorees

Ackerman, Diane. *Animal Sense* (Knopf Books for Young Readers)
Keyser, Samuel Jay. *The Pond God and Other Stories* (Front Street)
Myers, Walter Dean. *Blues Journey* (Holiday House)
Smith, Hope Anita. *The Way a Door Closes* (Henry Holt Books for Young Readers)

2003 Winner

Levy, Constance. *Splash! Poems of Our Watery World* (Orchard)

Honorees

Adoff, Jaime. *The Song Shoots Out of My Mouth* (Dutton Juvenile)

Testa, Maria. *Becoming Joe DiMaggio* (Candlewick)

Wayland, April Halprin. *Girl Coming in for a Landing: A Novel in Poems* (Alfred A. Knopf Books for Young Readers)

2002 Winner

Hines, Anna Grossnickle. *Pieces: A Year in Poems and Quilts* (Greenwillow)

Honorees

High, Linda Oatman. *A Humble Life: Plain Poems* (Wm. B. Eerdmans)

Smith, Charles R., Jr. *Short Takes: Fast-break Basketball Poetry* (Dutton)

2000 Honorees

Johnston, Tony. *An Old Shell: Poems of the Galapagos* (Farrar, Straus and Giroux Books for Young Readers)

Wong, Janet S. *The Rainbow Hand: Poems about Mothers and Children* (Margaret K. McElderry)

1999 Winner

Johnson, Angela. *The Other Side: The Shorter Poems* (Orchard)

1998 Winner

George, Kristine O'Connell. *The Great Frog Race and Other Poems* (Clarion)

1997 Winner

Bouchard, David. *Voices from the Wild* (Chronicle)

1996 Winner

Esbensen, Barbara Juster. *Dance with Me* (HarperCollins)

1995 Winner

Florian, Douglas. *Beast Feast* (Harcourt Brace)

1994 Winner

Wood, Nancy. *Spirit Walker* (Doubleday Books for Young Readers)

1993 Winner

Bryan, Ashley. *Sing to the Sun* (HarperCollins)

V. Lee Bennett Hopkins Promising Poet Award

2004

Johnson, Lindsay Lee. *Soul Moon Soup* (Front Street)

2001

Crist-Evans, Craig. *Moon Over Tennessee: A Boy's Civil War Journal* (Houghton Mifflin)

1998

George, Kristine O'Connell. *The Great Frog Race and Other Poems* (Clarion)

1995

Chandra, Deborah. *Rich Lizard and Other Poems* (Farrar, Straus and Giroux)

VI. The Lion and the Unicorn Award for Excellence in North American Poetry

2005 Winner

Nelson, Marilyn. *Fortune's Bones: The Manumission Requiem* (Front Street)

Honor Books

Frost, Helen. *Spinning through the Universe: A Novel in Poems from Room 214* (Farrar, Straus and Giroux)

Lawson, JonArno. *The Man in the Moon-fixer's Mask* (Pedlar)

Myers, Walter Dean. *Here in Harlem: Poems in Many Voices* (Holiday House)

Wolf, Allan. *New Found Land: Lewis & Clark's Voyage of Discovery* (Candlewick)

VII. Myra Cohn Livingston Award (Presented by the Children's Literature Council of Southern California)

2005

George, Kristine O'Connell. *Hummingbird Nest* (Harcourt)

2004

Smith, Hope Anita. *The Way a Door Closes* (Henry Holt Books for Young Readers)

2003

Wayland, April Halprin. *Girl Coming in for a Landing: A Novel in Poems* (Alfred A. Knopf Books for Young Readers)

2002

George, Kristine O'Connell. *Toasting Marshmallows: Camping Poems* (Clarion)

2000

Sones, Sonya. *Stop Pretending: What Happened When My Big Sister Went Crazy* (Harper Collins)

1999

George, Kristine O'Connell. *Old Elm Speaks: Tree Poems* (Houghton Mifflin)

VIII. Golden Kite Award (Presented by the Society of Children's Book Writers and Illustrators)

Honor Book 1995

Hopkins, Lee Bennett. *Been to Yesterdays: Poems of a Life* (Boyds Mills)

Honor Book 1982

Glenn, Mel. *Class Dismissed! High School Poems* (Clarion)

Honor Book 1981

Willard, Nancy. *A Visit to William Blake's Inn* (Harcourt)

Honor Book 1974

Livingston, Myra Cohn. *The Way Things Are, and Other Poems* (Atheneum)

IX. Claudia Louise Lewis Poetry Award (Presented by the Children's Book Committee at Bank Street College of Education)

2004

George, Kristine O'Connell. *Hummingbird Nest: A Journal of Poems* (Tricycle)

Myers, Walter Dean. *Here in Harlem: Poems in Many Voices* (Holiday House)

2003

Frame, Jeron Ashford. *Yesterday I Had the Blues* (Tricycle)

Smith, Hope Anita. *The Way a Door Closes* (Henry Holt Books for Young Readers)

2002

George, Kristine O'Connell. *Little Dog and Duncan* (Clarion)

2001

Creech, Sharon. *Love That Dog* (Joanna Cotler)

Williams, Vera B. *Amber Was Brave, Essie Was Smart* (Greenwillow)

2000

Florian, Douglas. *Mammalabilia* (Harcourt)

1999

Sones, Sonya. *Stop Pretending: What Happened When My Big Sister Went Crazy* (HarperCollins)

X. Flora Stieglitz Straus Award (Presented by the Children's Book Committee at Bank Street College of Education)

2001

Nelson, Marilyn. *Carver: A Life in Poems* (Front Street)

XI. NCTE Award for Poetry for Children

2003 Mary Ann Hoberman
2000 X. J. Kennedy
1997 Eloise Greenfield
1994 Barbara Juster Esbensen
1991 Valerie Worth
1988 Arnold Adoff
1985 Lilian Moore
1982 John Ciardi
1981 Eve Merriam
1980 Myra Cohn Livingston
1979 Karla Kuskin
1978 Aileen Fisher
1977 David McCord

Notes

Chapter 1

1. Blinded by the noontime sun, Frost was unable to read "For John F. Kennedy His Inauguration," which he had written for the occasion and was still in manuscript form. Exhausted from the day's events, Frost mistakenly called the president "Mr. John Finley," and despite Lyndon Johnson's attempt to shield the manuscript from the sun with his outstretched hat, Frost had to give up reading the poem. However, he recovered in style, reciting "The Gift Outright" from memory.

2. Many have argued that the relationship was only "apparent." For instance, when asked in a 1965 interview by A. Alvarez whether "some vague, fragile possibility of some kind of connection, even mutual interchange, between the representatives of the cultural life of the country and those of the world of power" had been encouraged by Kennedy, Robert Lowell responded,

> I was invited to the White House for [French minister of culture André] Malraux's dinner there [on May 11, 1962]. Kennedy made a rather graceful joke that "the White House was becoming almost a café for intellectuals . . ." Then we all drank a great deal at the White House, and had to sort of be told not to take our champagne into the concert, and to put our cigarettes out like children—though nicely, it wasn't peremptory. Then the next morning you read the Seventh Fleet had been sent somewhere in Asia and you had a funny feeling of how unimportant the artist really was; that this was sort of window dressing and that the real government was somewhere else, and that something much closer to the Pentagon was really ruling the country. (qtd. in Hamilton 299)

Earlier, in a May 31, 1962, letter to Edmund Wilson, Lowell articulated the same discomfort, writing that, save Wilson,

> everyone there seemed addled with adulation at having been invited. It was all good fun but next morning you read that the President has sent the 7th fleet to Laos, or he might have invaded Cuba again—not that he will, but I feel we intellectuals play a very pompous and frivolous role—we should be windows, not window-dressing. Then, now in our times, of all times, the sword hangs over us and our children, and not a voice is lifted. (*Letters* 409)

3. In the film *Frost at Michigan,* Frost called Robert Lowell, William Meredith, Richard Wilbur, and Donald Hall—all in the "cooked" camp—"his children" whom he "helped bring up" (qtd. in Meyers, *Frost* 297–98).

4. The appointment of the politically conservative Frost was a safe choice for the Fellows of the Library. Jarrell, it seems, was not such a safe choice. Mary Jarrell writes that shortly after Jarrell's appointment, Jarrell received a phone call from a rather "perturbed Basler," then the head of the reference department, who had received a report from "an unnamed informant [. . .] that Jarrell was a Communist" (*Letters* 408). Mary continues, saying Basler "cited the results of a McCarthyesque investigation that turned up (1) numerous poems and articles in such 'pinko publications' as *Partisan Review,* the *New Republic,* and *The Nation,* and (2) certain Marxist friendships at the University of Texas" (*Letters* 409). Though a reader of Marx, Jarrell was not and had never been a member of the Communist Party.

5. Golding lists the five anthologies, in order of publication: "Norman Foerster, ed., *American Poetry and Prose* (Boston: Houghton Mifflin, 1934); Jay B. Hubbell, ed., *American Life in Literature* (New York: Harper, 1936); the *Oxford* (New York: Oxford UP, 1938); Milton Ellis, Louise Pound, and George Weida Spohn, eds., *A College Book of American Literature,* vol. 2 (New York: American, 1940); and [Bernard] Smith's *The Democratic Spirit: A Collection of American Writings from the Earliest Times to the Present* (New York: Alfred A. Knopf, 1941)" (197). The other two poets who appeared in all five anthologies were Vachel Lindsay and Edna St. Vincent Millay.

6. Reviewing Ben Fuson's 1952 survey of "twenty-seven single and multivolume anthologies of American literature," Alan Golding writes, "The only modern American poets to appear in each of the fifteen multivolume anthologies examined were [Edwin Arlington] Robinson, Sandburg, and Frost [. . .] The only modern poet in every single-volume anthology was Frost again; the next highest level of representation went to Sandburg and Lindsay" (111).

7. See William Harmon's *The Concise Columbia Book of Poetry* (1990). In a 2003 interview poet laureate Billy Collins somewhat pessimistically notes, "There is one poem that has spoken to the American people, and that is 'Stopping by Woods on a Snowy Evening.' That is the most popular poem in America. It was either that or 'The Road Not Taken' that John F. Kennedy carried with him in his wallet on a piece of paper" (n.p.).

8. I will expound upon the distinctions between the "raw" and the "cooked" poetries of the late '50s and early '60s in chapter 2.

9. In his *Voices* essay, "The Poetry of Carl Sandburg," Henry W. Wells notes:

From the larger perspective, Sandburg has been both conservative and radical. On the one hand, he was in 1914 conservative chiefly in technique, for, much as his free verse departed from the traditions of stanza and rhyme, it made few radical changes from Whitman. His technique belongs more to advanced movements of the nineteenth century than to any movements whatsoever peculiar to the present century. On the other hand, he was in 1914 an innovator as regards his social imagination. (42)

10. For institutional histories of the New Criticism, I refer the reader to William Cain's *The Crisis in Criticism* and Gerald Graff's *Professing Literature.* Alan Golding also discusses the impact of New Criticism on formation of the American poetry canon in chapter 3 of his *From Outlaw to Classic: Canons in American Poetry.*

11. I will discuss Jarrell's theory of poetry at length in chapter 2.

12. In an interview for the *Paris Review,* Robert Penn Warren rejected the term "New Criticism" as being too vague to have any real meaning. Noting the methodological differences in approaches by New Critics such as "[I. A.] Richards, [T. S.] Eliot, [Allen] Tate, [Richard] Blackmur, [Yvor] Winters, [Cleanth] Brooks" and others, Warren points out that, ultimately,

> The term is, in one sense, a term without any referent—or with too many referents. It is a term that belongs to the conspiracy theory of history. A lot of people—chiefly aging, conservative professors scared of losing prestige, or young instructors afraid of not getting promoted, middle-brow magazine editors, and the flotsam and jetsam of semi-Marxist social-significance criticism left stranded by history—they all had a communal nightmare called the New Criticism to explain their vague discomfort. I think it was something they ate. (17–18)

13. In a letter to Alvin Dreier, Sandburg writes, "I am going to back Kennedy as against Nixon but I have taken an oath not to tear my shirt" (*Letters* 524). He kept both pledges and in June of 1961 wrote to Kennedy himself a dedicatory letter along with an inscribed copy of *Remembrance Rock.* In the letter Sandburg "salute[s]" Kennedy "on wonderfully appropriate appointments made and two speeches that are to become American classics" (537). In a September 1961 letter to Herbert Mitgang, Sandburg writes, seemingly without irony, "God help us all including the brave and forthright Jack Kennedy" (548). However, in 1960 Sandburg had less enthusiasm for Kennedy, and was only later to become, as Kennedy biographer Victor Lasky terms it, an "apologist-laureate of the New Frontier" (282). Lasky points to Bob Thomas's *Washington Star* piece "Candidates Feel Sting of Sandburg Evening," which quotes Sandburg characterizing Kennedy as "Merely a high-powered high-school boy. He's got more money than pleases some of us. Whether he has spent one or more millions to get the nomination would be interesting to know. The money is there for him through the quiet, smooth backing of his father, whose record gives some of us no elation" (282). If Kennedy had heard those words, they probably would not have ingratiated him to Sandburg.

14. After receiving the inscribed copy of Sandburg's *Remembrance Rock,* Kennedy wrote to Sandburg, "I have been an admirer of yours for many years and therefore I am extremely pleased to have this inscribed book" (qtd. in Sandburg, *Letters* 339).

15. Governor Adlai Stevenson used strikingly similar language to characterize Sandburg in a 1953 message taped for the poet's seventy-fifth birthday. Stevenson proclaims:

> Carl Sandburg is the one living man whose work and whose life epitomize the American dream. He has the earthiness of the prairies, the majesty of mountains, the anger of deep inland seas. In him is the restlessness of the seeker, the questioner, the explorer of far horizons, the hunger that is never satisfied. In him also is the tough strength that has never been fully measured, never unleashed, the resiliency of youthfulness which wells from within, and which no aging can destroy. (qtd. in Yannella xi)

16. Frost nurtured this image of himself. Jeffrey Meyers writes that Frost did "not intend to talk *about* American civilization" while visiting Israel in March of 1961, because, as Frost said, "*I* am American civilization" (qtd. in Meyers, *Frost* 325).

17. And there was a degree of condescension, perhaps even paternalism, in the relationship between those in power and poets. Of Frost's reading at the inauguration, Lasky writes, "Senator John Sparkman, Chairman of the Inaugural Committee, had introduced the eighty-six-year-old New Englander as a distinguished American poet 'who will recite an original composition,' an introduction which, to some of the invited intellectuals, smacked of a highschool [sic] exercise" (20).

18. The change was minor, though it does suggest a new frontier. Originally, the line read, "Such as she was, such as she would become." The revised line looks to the future, to future frontiers. This ending, evoking wild applause, gave the impression of improvisation: "Such as she was, such as she *would* become, *has* become, and I—and for this occasion let me change that to—what she *will* become" (Parini 414).

19. One would think Roethke would quibble with the placement of the heart of the United States in New England. As he writes in "Open Letter," "the marsh, the Void, is always in [Michigan], immediate and terrifying. It is a splendid place for schooling the spirit. It is America" (70).

20. Curiously, in Marilyn Fain Apseloff's *They Wrote for Children Too: An Annotated Bibliography of Children's Literature by Famous Writers for Adults,* Frost's last book, *In the Clearing,* is listed as a work for children. She writes, "These are not the usual, familiar Frost poems found in editions for children, for these are far more difficult in language and references" (119). This is to be expected, as *In the Clearing* was a new collection intended for adult readers, not children. Frost's association with child readers, particularly of high school age, probably accounts for Apseloff's confusion. "The Gift Outright" and "For John F. Kennedy His Inauguration" appear in the collection.

21. Note that Arbuthnot uses Frost's original final line.

22. Langston Hughes also read at the festival. Brooks, however, read on the second day, October 23, whereas Hughes read on the twenty-fourth, directly preceding Jarrell. An admirer of Hughes, Jarrell joked before beginning his reading, "It is hard to come after Mr. Hughes" (*National* 209).

23. As we shall see in chapter 3, true poetry of the playground—those poems composed and performed by children in the absence of adults—is generally much more profane, disruptive, and subversive than the poetry exemplified by the work of Shel Silverstein and his peers, writers of what I call domesticated playground poetry.

Chapter 2

1. In "The Other Frost" (1947), for example, Jarrell complicated the popular conception of Robert Frost, arguing that beneath Frost's seemingly tranquil poetry there lies a dark undercurrent, intensifying Frost's reputation. Jarrell also charted with amazing acumen the poetic landscape of twentieth-century American poetry in his talk "50 Years of American Poetry" at the 1962 National Poetry Festival, a lecture well attended by prominent critics and poets (and reprinted in his *The Third Book*

of Criticism [1963]). In *Poetry's Catbird Seat,* William McGuire quotes Karl Shapiro's reflection on the talk: "All the poets sat on the edge of their seats while Jarrell, who everybody had to admit had earned the right to do so, put together the jigsaw puzzle of modern poetry in front of our eyes. When I was finally fitted into place, with a splash of color, I felt a relief that I fitted, and a regret that the puzzle had been solved" (239).

Jarrell also reinvigorated the failing reputation of Walt Whitman. In "Some Lines from Whitman," an essay requested by John Crowe Ransom for the *Kenyon Review* (reprinted in *Poetry and the Age* [1953]), Jarrell, in the words of William Prichard, "immortalizes lines by Whitman which, ever and only since his essay celebrated them, have been quoted and requoted" (212–13).

2. X. J. Kennedy argues that Ciardi "was responsible to a large extent" for the "change in climate" that allowed poets for adults to write children's verse without shame (*Reason* 61).

3. Lowell is a bit more candid in his assessment of the "raw" poets—Gregory Corso, Allen Ginsberg, and Peter Orlovsky, in particular—in an April 7, 1959, letter to Elizabeth Bishop. The paragraph in question warrants quoting in full:

> The other night Ginsberg, Corso and Orlovsky came to call on me. As you know[,] our house, as Lizzie says, is nothing if not pretentious. Planned to stun such people. When they came in, they all took off their wet shoes and tiptoed upstairs. They are phony in [a] way because they have made a lot of publicity out of very little talent. But in another way, they are pathetic and doomed. How can you make a go for long by reciting so-so verse to half-jeering swarms of college students? However, they are trying, I guess[,] to write poetry. They are fairly easy to listen to. There was an awful lot of subdued talk about their being friends and lovers, and once Ginsberg and Orlovsky disappeared in unison to the john and reappeared on each other's shoulders. I haven't had the heart to tell this to Lizzie or anyone else. They also talked a lot about entering the lion's cave, a reference, I think, to my "David and Bathsheba." I think they'll die of TB. (*Letters* 343)

Several days earlier, in a letter to Ginsberg, Lowell discusses the experimental magazine *Big Table,* which was formed, among other reasons, to make public the suppressed contents of a 1959 issue of the *Chicago Review.* In this letter Lowell calls Edward Dahlberg "a tremendous and good writer," but goes on to characterize Jack Kerouac as an "uninspired Joyce." He finds "Burroughs very real, but partially of psycho-pathic interest," and—like Jarrell—approves of Corso (with a few caveats): "[He] is good in some of the short poems you name in your preface, and say, 'Dolls.' [. . .] Corso is a small attractive poet, not in the same universe as Williams, or Moore or Pound or many others that I like, such as Auden." Finally, Lowell comments on the court case between the U.S. Post Office and *Big Table* (concerning the mailabilty of the magazine, as it was potentially obscene), concluding, "I can't see why *Big Table* should be suppressed, it strikes me as perfectly moral and serious" (342).

4. Juliana Spahr notes in *Everybody's Autonomy* that language writing, while sharing the leftist leanings and formal experimentation of the New American school, differs fundamentally in its theoretical underpinnings. The New American school "speaks against the system, yet remains voice- and personality-centered" (57),

whereas language writing is generally "anti-individualistic and anti-ego-centered" (73).

5. Thought to be lost, "Levels and Opposites" was a *Mesures* lecture given by Jarrell at Princeton University in April 1942 at the request of Allen Tate. Travisano rediscovered the essay in the midst of Jarrell's papers, and it was subsequently published in the winter 1996 issue of the *Georgia Review.*

6. See chapter 1 for a discussion of the New Criticism.

7. For discussions of the scenic mode and voice-lyric traditions, see Charles Altieri, *Self and Sensibility in Contemporary American Poetry* (1984), chapter 2; Charles Bernstein, "The Academy in Peril: William Carlos Williams Meets the MLA," reprinted in his *Contents Dream* (1986); and Hank Lazer, *Opposing Poetries* (1996), vol. 1, chapter 1.

8. I will discuss at length the various modes prevalent in contemporary American children's poetry in chapters 3 and 4.

9. Note that poetries that give voice to other, marginalized voices call into question the "class dialect" constructed by the dominant mode of poetry. The poems of Langston Hughes, Gwendolyn Brooks, June Jordan, and Nikki Giovanni, for example, implicitly interrogate the dominant poetic voice, which, as Easthope argues, is a bourgeois class dialect, even as they sometimes employ the pentameter.

10. This paradox is also apparent in the raw poets of the 1950s and '60s. For example, even as Koch lambastes the intellectual poets of the academy (and let's remember, Koch was a professor at Columbia and a student of Harvard), he is also implicated in that tradition, steeped in "the great poets of our time . . . / Yeats of the baleful influence, Auden of the baleful influence, Eliot of the baleful influence," (Allen 231).

11. In the middle of the reading, Ginsberg, ever the iconoclast, leapt up and shouted, "Coupla squares yakking!" According to Mary Jarrell, "Jarrell finished the poem and was finished with Ginsberg" (qtd. in *Letters* 418).

12. This poem, along with "The Chipmunk's Day," appeared in the *New Yorker,* and of the pair Jarrell said, "[They] were pretty much like grown-up poems—anyway, *The New Yorker* printed them. I didn't tell them they were children's poems" (qtd. in Mary Jarrell, *Remembering* 101).

13. Mary Jarrell explicitly ties this scene to Jarrell's biography, noting, "This minor episode [. . .] came from Randall's attempt to write a book on Hart Crane for Holt and Company. Although Randall admired Crane, was extremely interested in him, and had accepted a $2,000 advance to write about him, he could not" (*Remembering* 102–03).

Chapter 3

1. Though a considerable body of work surrounds playground poetry, it treats children's playground rhymes exclusively as folklore and, for the most part, consists of collecting rhymes and annotating sources. One of the most notable early studies of children's poetry and song as folklore is Iona and Peter Opie's *I Saw Esau: Traditional Rhymes of Youth* (1947), followed by their equally important *The Lore and Language of Schoolchildren* (1959), the first book in a trilogy of texts including *Children's Games in Street and Playground* (1969) and *The Singing Game* (1985). These studies,

generally ethnographic and anecdotal, do not consider the rhymes *as poetry,* as rich, complicated—if ribald and irreverent—poems that deserve analysis from a literary perspective. In *The People in the Playground* (1993), Iona Opie writes that in these books she and her husband "tried to demonstrate the quantity, diversity, and astonishing longevity of children's lore," which includes their poetry, games, and riddles (viii). However, the Opies only implicitly suggest the literary merit of the poetry of childhood, generally sidestepping its political dimension, which, as we will see when we discuss anti- and pro-integration rhymes, is considerable.

Francelia Butler's *Skipping Around the World: The Ritual Nature of Folk Rhymes* (1989) is another interesting work that amasses and annotates a great number of rhymes. *Skipping* is in the spirit of its predecessors: *Jump-Rope Rhymes* (1970), by Roger D. Abrahams; *One Potato, Two Potato: The Folklore of American Children* (1976), by Mary and Herbert Knapp; and *Counting Out Rhymes* (1980), by Abrahams and Lois Rankin. These texts implicitly question romantic notions of the innocent child, pointing to the complicated social systems generated in children's play, emphasizing the child's desire to make sense out of (and often to lampoon) so-called adult concerns like sex and violence. In *Jump-Rope Rhymes* Abrahams articulates his dissatisfaction with the contemporary study of children's rhymes, specifically jumping rhymes: "Commentary on jumping rope has been done primarily by journalist and recreation experts," he complains, noting that much of the commentary "has been of the 'isn't this cute' sort" (xix). He then remarks on the paucity of rigorous, historical investigations into "the ways in which [playground rhymes] fit [. . .] into other patterns of play activity" (xix). In the years since Abrahams wrote these words, considerable work has been done in this area (notably by the Knapps). But most of the literature still operates in the presentational mode. Indeed, one of the latest books on children's rhyme as folklore, Josepha Sherman and T. K. F. Weisskopf's excellent *Greasy Grimy Gopher Guts: The Subversive Folklore of Childhood* (1995), resembles, like Butler's, an annotated anthology of collected rhymes and songs. Of the book-length studies concerning the oral folk-poetry of children, *Greasy Grimy Gopher Guts* and *One Potato, Two Potato* are the most useful and exhaustive treatments of the oral folk-poetry of contemporary U.S. children. Though my goal is not to treat these rhymes as folklore, I sympathize with Abrahams's critique and seek in this chapter to extend the parameters of the discourse surrounding playground rhymes—again, not as folklore, but as a dense poetic tradition consisting of equally dense and rewarding texts.

2. The 1992 edition, marvelously illustrated by Maurice Sendak, is obviously designed to appeal to children.

3. Chaston's thoughts on Baum's *Oz* books appear in his "Baum, Bakhtin, and Broadway: A Centennial Look at the Carnival of Oz," *Lion and the Unicorn* 25.1: 128–49.

4. Though these two rhymes actually work well together as a two-stanza poem, they are in fact separate rhymes.

5. I remember hearing the rhyme as "Miss Suzy," though many of my students remember "Ms. Lucy." Other versions outline the exploits of Ms. (or Miss) Helen, Lulu, Mary, Rosie, Sally, Suzanne, and even Johnny. Given the content of the poem, Ms. Lucy, with its pun on the word *loose,* is perhaps the most appropriate of the

list. For a brief but enlightening history of the rhyme, see Sherman and Weisskopf, pages 205–07.

6. Some children might not appreciate the embedded profanities in "Ms. Lucy," but I imagine those children are rare and principally the production of the naïve adult's imagination. As Butler writes of skipping rhymes in general: "I have heard adults protest that children could not have made up most of these rhymes because they do not understand the sexual implications. However, since we know that children manifest erotic behavior from birth, there is reason to believe that many of them are fully aware and capable of imagining without any adult assistance the rhymes they are chanting" (57).

Chapter 4

1. Livingston takes the name "garbage delight" from the title of Canadian poet Dennis Lee's 1977 collection, *Garbage Delight*.

2. For instance, see Livingston's essay "The Poem on Page 81" (214, 223), her book *Child as Poet: Myth or Reality?* (165, 172–73, 200–201, 287), and the introduction to "David McCord's Poems."

3. This mode of poetry should perhaps more fairly be called urchin *poetry*, for, as John Hollander writes in *Rhyme's Reason, verse* simply connotes the "surface patterns of words" (1). Hollander is not alone in thinking "most verse is not poetry," a sometimes useful distinction. However, to avoid diminishing this particular mode of children's poetry, I will modify Townsend's terminology to *urchin poetry*.

4. *Words for the Wind* was published in England a year earlier than in the United States, thus the date of this essay.

5. See their essay "From the Editors: Cross-Writing and the Reconceptualizing of Children's Literary Studies," *Children's Literature* 25 (1997).

6. Geisel became the author head of Beginner Books in 1960.

7. Jack Prelutsky performs a similar, though larger scale, rewriting in his *A Nonny Mouse* books (1989, 1996), which attribute anonymous poems (and some of Prelutsky's own) to a little mouse. The most recent contribution to this series, *A Nonny Mouse Writes Again: Poems* (1999), features, along with Prelutsky, the talents of Harry Mazer.

8. Travisano writes:

> Roethke was similarly preoccupied with selfhood, loss, the wonder and darkness of childhood, and a long-term experiment with dreamlike textures. Still, Lowell, Jarrell, Bishop, and Berryman each felt that Roethke's work, even as they admired it, evinced a markedly different sensibility. Put simply, they found Roethke's work significantly more romantic. Roethke, they believed, was more deliberately lyric and sensuous, more emotionally expansive, and also, they appear to have felt, less searchingly self-critical and self-ironic. (*Midcentury* 19)

9. Though line 11 is printed as two lines in *I Am! Says the Lamb* ("You asked me before, / I'll tell you again"), it appears as one line in *Dirty Dinky and Other Creatures* as well as in Roethke's collected poems.

10. See chapter 2 for a discussion of Jarrell's position on modern poetry and romanticism.

11. Silverstein is both an adult cartoonist who has penned comics and rhymes for *Playboy* and a popular songwriter. ("A Boy Named Sue," sung by Johnny Cash, is one of his most well-known songs.)

12. Silverstein, however, undercuts the ostensible didacticism apparent in some of his poems by cultivating the public persona of a hard-drinking bad boy. For an extended discussion of Silverstein's public persona and the ways in which this persona complicates and extends his children's poetry, see my essay "Reappraising Uncle Shelby" (283–93) in the May/June 2005 special poetry issue of the *Horn Book Magazine.*

13. However, as I argue in "Reappraising Uncle Shelby," one might read these "rolls on the rug" as something more akin to an orgiastic roll in the hay than a simple "hug." My friend Caroline Jones pointed out this possibility to me. I missed it for the longest time, as I'm sure many of Silverstein's adult readers do, reducing the poem to mere sentimentality. Of course, not everyone misses this possibility: the Polyamory Society (a nonprofit organization promoting multipartner relationships and families) quotes the entirety of Silverstein's poem on their Web site (http://www.polyamorysociety.org/), although they mistitle the poem "Everyone Wins" and format the poem incorrectly.

14. "I Got Stoned and I Missed It" appears on *Freakin' at the Freakers Ball* (1973). "Fuck 'Em" and "I Love My Right Hand" appear on an undated bootleg, found at A&R Recording Studio, New York, which has been circulating among fans for some years now. Various fan sites on the Internet hold that the demo dates from the late '60s or early '70s. Two excellent online resources for Silverstein-related issues, including the dating of this demo, are Sarah Weinman's *The Shel Silverstein Archive* (http://members.tripod.com/~ShelSilverstein/) and *Shel Silverstein's Adult Works* at www.banned-width.com.

15. Even if they could purchase it, sadly, *Greasy Grimy Gopher Guts* is, as of this writing, out of print, an unfortunate development for such a noteworthy text.

Chapter 5

1. Most readers will be familiar with Lewis Carroll's "A Mouse's Tale" as it appears in *Alice's Adventures in Wonderland.* However, Carroll included a different mouse poem in the manuscript version of *Alice's Adventures Under Ground,* a hand lettered novel written and illustrated for Alice Liddell. This version, modeled on the oral tale he famously narrated to Alice and her two sisters on their much-discussed July 4, 1862, boat trip, was begun the day after their journey, although he did not present it to young Alice until November 26, 1864 (by which time he was already reworking the novel into the version published as *Alice's Adventures in Wonderland*). In 1885 he borrowed Alice's copy to produce a facsimile edition. The hand-drawn mouse poem from that edition is a direct precursor to the hand-drawn calligrams of Guillaume Apollinaire, published in his posthumous collection *Calligrammes: Poèmes de la paix et de la guerre 1913–1916* (1918), particularly "La Fiue l'oeillet et la pipe à opium" and "Madeleine." Carroll's later mouse poem, using typed letters as it does, resembles Apollinaire's typed experiments, such as "Il pleut" and "Paysage." For reference, I reproduce the mouse poem from *Alice's Adventures Under Ground* here:

We lived beneath the mat
Warm and snug and fat
But one woe, & that
Was the cat!
To our joys
a clog, In
our eyes a
fog, On our
hearts a log
Was the dog!
When the
Cat's away,
Then
The mice
will
play,
But, alas!
one day, (So they say)
Came the dog and
cat, Hunting
for a
rat,
Crushed
the mice
all flat,
Each
one
as
he
sat
Underneath the mat,— Think of that!

2. According to Mario A. Di Cesare, each "wing" was "printed vertically in the 1633 edition (but horizontally in the manuscripts)" (16). Since vertical printing is typographically more demanding, most editions since have printed the stanzas horizontally. The vertical alignment, however, is more visually interesting, more immediately summoning to mind the image of wings.

3. Higgins remarks briefly on Vendler's impatience with the visual dimension of poetry, noting her treatment of George Herbert's "Easter Wings," in which she "prints and analyzes it without even noting its visual aspect, let alone its tradition (the parallel with the Hellenist Greek wings of Simias, etc.)" (*Pattern Poetry* 16).

4. Curiously, McCord himself has experimented with typography and visual

elements in his poetry, particularly in "The Grasshopper" in *Far and Few* (1952) and "Summer Shower" in *For Me to Say* (1970). Myra Cohn Livingston also finds occasion to employ the techniques she decries in this essay. *O Sliver of Liver* (1979) contains several visual pieces, including "Winter Tree" and "Piano Lesson (Carissa)." Furthermore, Livingston's "4-Way Stop," which is anthologized by the Kennedys in *Knock at a Star,* uses found elements.

5. Though not marketed as a collection of children's poetry, Maira Kalman's exceptional picture book *Max Makes a Million* (1990), about a dog poet who yearns for Paris, is another compelling example of the productive interface between graphic design and text.

6. See my essay, "Mel Glenn and Arnold Adoff: The Poetics of Power in the Adolescent Voice-lyric," in *Style* 35.3 (2001): 486–97.

7. Besides "Concrete Cat," two other poems have been attributed to Dorthi Charles. One, an untitled haiku, appears in *Knock at a Star;* the other, "Getting Dirty," appears in Dorothy and X. J. Kennedy's popular anthology for young children, *Talking Like the Rain: A Read-to-Me Book of Poems* (1992). "Getting Dirty" differs quite significantly from "Concrete Cat," resembling more closely Kennedy's signed children's poems in its concern with aural effects. I quote from the first of its six stanzas: "Let's go rolling, rolling / Fast as round rocks roll / Down a hillside, hollering / When we hit a hole."

8. Of course, Kennedy is not the first to attack visual poetry with parody. Dick Higgins reminds us that Johann Bernhard Frisch (1666–1743) "attacked pattern poetry in part by doing it" (*Pattern Poetry* 14). Like Kennedy's parody, Frisch's work was more successful than he intended: "The resulting pieces [. . .] are the only pieces by him that are remembered today—especially the one that is shaped like the Bear of Berlin [. . .] which can still be bought in souvenir stalls in that city" (14).

9. Goodrich's rhyme was revived by Maurice Sendak in *Higglety Pigglety Pop! Or, There Must Be More to Life* (1967).

Coda

1. The other two titles, incidentally, consist of an anthology, *Reflections on a Gift of Watermelon Pickle . . . ,* and Dr. Seuss's prose fairy tale *The Five Hundred Hats of Bartholomew Cubbins.*

2. Untermeyer's anthology is now called *Golden Book's Family Treasury of Poetry.*

3. Another outcome of this state of affairs has been the publication of more anthologies like Harold Bloom's *Stories and Poems for Extremely Intelligent Children of All Ages* (2001), whose contents are completely in the public domain.

4. See appendix A for a complete list of the poets with at least three poems in any one of the selected anthologies. Appendix B lists these poets by nationality.

5. None of the other anthologies surveyed include poetry by Untermeyer, however, whereas nine poems with his name appear in *The Golden Treasury*. Add to this nine the three poems attributed to Michael Lewis, Untermeyer's pseudonym, and his total rises to twelve, making him the best-represented poet in the anthology. In terms of self-representation, only Jack Prelutsky, whose anthology features twenty-eight pieces of his own work, tops Untermeyer.

6. Ciardi's *Mid-Century American Poetry* and the pedagogical impulse inform-
ing it are discussed in chapter 4.

7. Though "Concrete Cat" is credited to Dorthi Charles, X. J. Kennedy is the
author. See chapter 5 for a discussion of the poem.

8. Considering John Ciardi's failing reputation and current critical standing,
which is a subtext of Edward M. Cifelli's excellent biography, Ciardi's absence from
Sword and McCarthy's anthology is not surprising.

9. A complete list of the most well-represented U.S. poets and their poems
can be found in appendix C.

Works Cited

Abbott, Craig S. "Modern American Poetry: Anthologies, Classroom, and Canons." *College Literature* 17.2–3 (1990): 209–21.

Abrahams, Roger D., ed. *Jump-Rope Rhymes: A Dictionary.* Austin: U of Texas P, 1969.

———. *Positively Black.* Englewood Cliffs, NJ: Prentice Hall, 1970.

Adoff, Arnold. *Slow Dance Heart Break Blues.* New York: Lothrop, Lee and Shepard, 1995.

Allen, Donald, ed. *New American Poetry, 1945–1960.* New York: Grove, 1960.

Altieri, Charles. *Self and Sensibility in Contemporary American Poetry.* Cambridge: Cambridge UP, 1984.

Applewhite, James. "Poetry and Value: A Personal View." *South Atlantic Quarterly* 90.3 (1991): 469–81.

Apseloff, Marilyn F. *They Wrote for Children Too: An Annotated Bibliography of Children's Literature by Famous Writers for Adults.* New York: Greenwood, 1989.

Arbuthnot, May H. *Children and Books.* Rev. ed. Chicago: Scott, Foresman, 1957.

———. *Children and Books.* 3rd ed. Chicago: Scott, Foresman, 1964.

Bakhtin, Mikhail. *Rabelais and His World.* Trans. Hélène Iswolsky. Bloomington: Indiana UP, 1984.

Barthes, Roland. *S/Z.* Trans. Richard Miller. New York: Hill and Wang, 1974.

Basler, Roy. *The Muse and the Librarian.* Westport, CT: Greenwood, 1974.

Berger, John. *Ways of Seeing.* New York: Penguin Books, 1977.

Bernstein, Charles. "Against National Poetry Month as Such." April 1999. March 3, 2003 <http://www.press.uchicago.edu/Misc/Chicago/044106.html>.

———. *Content's Dream: Essays, 1975–1984.* Los Angeles: Sun and Moon, 1986.

Bloom, Harold, ed. *Stories and Poems for Extremely Intelligent Children of All Ages.* New York: Scribner, 2001.

Bohn, Willard. *Aesthetics of Visual Poetry, 1914–1928.* New York: Cambridge UP, 1986.

———. *Apollinaire and the International Avant-garde.* Albany: State U of New York P, 1997.

———. *The Dada Market: An Anthology of Poetry.* Carbondale: Southern Illinois UP, 1993.

———. *Modern Visual Poetry.* Newark: U of Delaware P, 2001.

Bridges, Ruby. *Through My Eyes: Ruby Bridges.* New York: Scholastic, 1999.

Brooks, Gwendolyn. *Bronzeville Boys and Girls.* New York: Harper, 1956.

———. "Poets who are Negroes." *Phylon* 11 (1950): 312.

———. *Report from Part One.* Detroit: Broadside, 1973.

Brunner, Edward. *Cold War Poetry.* Urbana: U of Illinois P, 2001.

Butler, Francelia. *Skipping Around the World.* Hamden: Library Professional Publications, 1989.

Cain, William E. *The Crisis in Criticism: Theory, Literature, and Reform in English Studies.* Baltimore: Johns Hopkins UP, 1984.

Carroll, Lewis. *Alice's Adventures in Wonderland.* New York: Knoff, 1984.

———. *Alice's Adventures Under Ground.* New York: Macmillan, 1932.

Ciardi, John, ed. *I Met a Man.* Boston: Houghton Mifflin, 1961.

———. *Mid-Century American Poets.* New York: Twayne, 1950.

———. *The Monster Den: Or Look What Happened at My House—and to It.* Honesdale: Wordsong, 1991.

———. *The Reason for the Pelican.* Honesdale: Wordsong, 1994.

———. *The Selected Letters of John Ciardi.* Ed. Edward M. Cifelli. Fayetteville: U of Arkansas P, 1991.

———. *You Know Who.* Honesdale: Wordsong, 1991.

———. *You Read to Me, I'll Read to You.* New York: Harper Trophy, 1987.

Cifelli, Edward M. *John Ciardi: A Biography.* Fayetteville: U of Arkansas P, 1997.

Clark, Beverly L. "Thirteen Ways of Thumbing your Nose at Children's Literature." *Lion and the Unicorn* 16.2 (1992): 240–44.

Collins, Billy. Interview with Regan Good. "Versus Verses." *New York Times.* Feb. 23, 2003 <http://www.nytimes.com/2003/02/23/magazine/23QUESTIONS.html?tntemail1>.

Coontz, Stephanie. *The Way We Never Were: American Families and the Nostalgia Trap.* New York: Basic Books, 1992.

Creech, Sharon. "Inspiration." March 3, 2003 <http://www.sharoncreech.co.uk/inspri.asp>.

———. *Love That Dog.* New York: HarperCollins, 2001.

DeCandido, GraceAnne A. Rev. of *Doodle Dandies: Poems That Take Shape,* by J. Patrick Lewis. *Booklist.* July 1998: 1876.

Denman, Gregory A. *When You've Made It Your Own . . . Teaching Poetry to Young People.* Portsmouth, NH: Heinemann, 1988.

Di Cesare, Mario A., ed. *George Herbert and the Seventeenth-Century Religious Poets.* New York: Norton, 1978.

Dickey, James. "Randall Jarrell." *Randall Jarrell, 1914–1965.* Ed. Robert Lowell, Peter Taylor, and Robert Penn Warren. New York: Farrar, Straus and Giroux, 1967.

Dryden, John. *Selected Poetry and Prose of John Dryden.* Ed. Earl Miner. New York: Random House, 1985.

Dunning, Stephen, Edward Lueders, and Hugh Smith, eds. *Reflections on a Gift of Watermelon Pickle . . . and Other Modern Verse.* Glenview, IL: Scott, Foresman, 1966.

Easthope, Antony. *Poetry as Discourse.* New York: Methuen, 1983.

Egoff, Sheila, et al., eds. *Only Connect: Readings on Children's Literature.* 3rd ed. Toronto: Oxford UP, 1996.

Ferguson, Suzanne. *The Poetry of Randall Jarrell.* Baton Rouge: Louisiana State UP,

1971.

Flynn, Richard. "Can Children's Poetry Matter?" *Lion and the Unicorn* 17.1 (1993): 37–44.

———. "'The Kindergarten of New Consciousness': Gwendolyn Brooks and the Social Construction of Childhood." *African American Review* 34.3 (2000): 483–99.

———. *Randall Jarrell and the Lost World of Childhood.* Athens: U of Georgia P, 1990.

Foucault, Michel. *This Is Not a Pipe.* Trans. James Harkness. Berkeley: U of California P, 1983.

Freud, Sigmund. *The Interpretation of Dreams.* Trans. James Strachey. New York: Avon Books, 1998.

———. *Three Essays on the Theory of Sexuality.* Trans. James Strachey. Rev. ed. New York: Basic Books, 2000.

———. "The 'Uncanny.'" *The Pelican Freud Library: On Art and Literature.* Ed. Albert Dickson. Vol. 14. Harmondsworth, UK: Penguin, 1985. 335–76.

Frost, Robert. *Collected Poems, Prose and Plays.* New York: Library of America, 1995.

———. "Education by Poetry." *Selected Prose of Robert Frost.* Ed. Hyde Cox and Edward Connery Lathem. New York: Holt, Rinehart and Winston, 1966.

———. *Poetry and Prose.* Ed. Edward C. Lathem and Lawrance Thompson. New York: Holt, Rinehart and Winston, 1972.

Gates, Henry L., Jr. *Signifying Monkey: A Theory of Afro-American Literary Criticism.* New York: Oxford UP, 1988.

Golding, Alan. *From Outlaw to Classic: Canons in American Poetry.* Madison: U of Wisconsin P, 1995.

Graff, Gerald. *Professing Literature: An Institutional History.* Chicago: U of Chicago P, 1987.

Gray, Donald J., ed. *Alice in Wonderland.* By Lewis Carroll. 2nd ed. New York: Norton, 1992.

Gray, Richard. *American Poetry of the Twentieth Century.* New York: Longman, 1990.

Greenway, William, and Betty Greenway. "Meeting the Muse: Teaching Contemporary Poetry by Teaching Poetry Writing." *Children's Literature Association Quarterly* 15.3 (1990): 138–42.

Griswold, Jerome. *The Children's Books of Randall Jarrell.* Athens: U of Georgia P, 1988.

Hall, Donald, ed. *The Oxford Book of Children's Poetry in America.* New York: Oxford UP, 1985.

———, ed. *The Oxford Illustrated Book of American Children's Poems.* Oxford: Oxford UP, 1999.

Hall, Donald, Robert Pack, and Louis Simpson, eds. *New Poets of England and America.* New York: Meridian Books, 1957.

Hamilton, Ian. *Robert Lowell: A Biography.* New York: Random House, 1982.

Harmon, William. *The Concise Columbia Book of Poetry.* New York: Columbia UP, 1990.

Hejinian, Lyn. "The Rejection of Closure." *Writing/talks.* Ed. Bob Perelman.

Carbondale: Southern Illinois UP, 1984. 270–91.

Heyman, Michael. "A New Defense of Nonsense; or, Where Then Is His Phallus? and Other Questions Not to Ask." *Children's Literature Association Quarterly* 24.4 (1999–2000): 187–94.

Higgins, Dick. *Horizons: The Poetics and Theory of the Intermedia.* Carbondale: Southern Illinois UP, 1984.

———. *Pattern Poetry: Guide to an Unknown Literature.* Albany: State U of New York P, 1987.

Hollander, John. *Rhyme's Reason: A Guide to English Verse.* New enlarged ed. New Haven, CT: Yale UP, 1989.

Holquist, Michael. Prologue. *Rabelais and His World.* By Mikhail Bakhtin. Trans. Hélène Iswolsky. Bloomington: Indiana UP, 1984. xiii–xxiii.

Homer, William Innes. *Alfred Stieglitz and the American Avant-garde.* Boston: New York Graphic Society, 1977.

Hopkins, Lee Bennett, ed. *My America: A Poetry Atlas of the United States.* New York: Scholastic, 2000.

Huck, Charlotte S., Susan Helper, and Janet Hickman. *Children's Literature in the Elementary School.* 5th ed. New York: Harcourt Brace Jovanovich, 1993.

Janeczko, Paul B. *A Poke in the I: A Collection of Concrete Poems.* Cambridge: Candlewick, 2001.

Jarrell, Mary. "The Group of Two." *Randall Jarrell, 1914–1965.* Ed. Robert Lowell, Peter Taylor, and Robert Penn Warren. New York: Farrar, Straus and Giroux, 1967. 274–98.

———. Introduction. *The Children's Books of Randall Jarrell.* By Jerome Griswold. Athens: U of Georgia P, 1988. 1–22.

———. *Remembering Randall: A Memoir of Poet, Critic, and Teacher.* New York: HarperCollins, 1999.

Jarrell, Randall. *The Bat-Poet.* New York: Macmillan, 1964.

———. *The Complete Poems.* New York: Farrar, Straus and Giroux, 1969.

———. "The End of the Line." *Kipling, Auden, & Co.: Essays and Reviews, 1935–1964.* New York: Farrar, Straus and Giroux, 1980. 76–83.

———. "Fifty Years of American Poetry." *The Third Book of Criticism.* New York: Farrar, Straus and Giroux, 1969. 295–334.

———. "Good Fences Make Good Poets." *Kipling, Auden, & Co.: Essays and Reviews, 1935–1964.* New York: Farrar, Straus and Giroux, 1980. 365–68.

———. "Levels and Opposites: Structure in Poetry." *Georgia Review* 50.4 (1996): 697–713.

———. *The Lost World.* New York: Macmillan, 1965.

———. "A Note on Poetry." *Kipling, Auden, & Co.: Essays and Reviews, 1935–1964.* New York: Farrar, Straus and Giroux, 1980. 47–51.

———. "Poetry, Unlimited." *Kipling, Auden, & Co.: Essays and Reviews, 1935–1964.* New York: Farrar, Straus and Giroux, 1980. 157–61.

———. "Poets, Critics, and Readers." *Kipling, Auden, & Co.: Essays and Reviews, 1935–1964.* New York: Farrar, Straus and Giroux, 1980. 305–18.

———. *Randall Jarrell's Letters.* Ed. Mary Jarrell. Boston: Houghton Mifflin, 1985.

Joseph, Stephen M., ed. *The Me Nobody Knows: Children's Voices from the Ghetto.* New

York: World, 1969.

Kennedy, John F. "Remarks Recorded for the Television Program 'Robert Frost: American Poet.' February 26, 1961." *Public Papers of the Presidents of the United States: John F. Kennedy. Containing the Public Messages, Speeches, and Statements of the President, January 20 to December 31, 1961.* Washington, DC: United States Government Printing Office, 1962. 125.

Kennedy, X. J. Afterword. *The Reason for the Pelican.* By John Ciardi. Honesdale: Boyds Mill, 1994. 61–64.

———. "Strict and Loose Nonsense." *Only Connect: Readings on Children's Literature.* 3rd ed. Ed. Sheila Egoff, et al. Toronto: Oxford UP, 1996. 225–35.

Kennedy, X. J., and Dorothy Kennedy. *Instructor's Manual: An Introduction to Poetry.* 7th ed. Glenview, IL: Little, Brown, 1990.

———. *Knock at a Star: A Child's Introduction to Poetry.* New York: Little, Brown, 1982.

———. *Knock at a Star: A Child's Introduction to Poetry.* Rev. ed. New York: Little, Brown, 1999.

———. *Talking Like the Rain: A Read-to-Me Book of Poems.* New York: Little, Brown, 1992.

King, Doris M. "The Feeling and Texture of Childness." Rev. of *Bronzeville Boys and Girls,* by Gwendolyn Brooks. *Phylon* 18 (First Quarter 1957): 93–94.

Knoepflmacher, U. C., and Mitzi Myers. "From the Editors: Cross-Writing and the Reconceptualizing of Children's Literary Studies." *Children's Literature* 25 (1997): vii–xvii.

Koch, Kenneth. *Rose, Where Did You Get that Red? Teaching Great Poetry to Children.* New York: Random House, 1973.

———. *Wishes, Lies, and Dreams: Teaching Children to Write Poetry.* New York: HarperCollins, 1999.

Koch, Kenneth, and Kate Farrell, eds. *Talking to the Sun: An Illustrated Anthology of Poems for Young People.* New York: Henry Holt, 1985.

Koch, Kenneth, and Phillip Lopate. "Interview with Kenneth Koch." *Journal of a Living Experiment: A Documentary History of the First Ten Years of Teachers and Writers Collaborative.* Ed. Phillip Lopate. New York: Teachers and Writers, 1979. 269–81.

Langbaum, Robert. "The New Nature Poetry." *American Scholar* 28.3 (1959): 323–40.

Lasky, Victor. *J.F.K.: The Man and the Myth.* New York: Macmillan, 1963.

Lazer, Hank. *Opposing Poetries.* Vol. 1. *Issues and Institutions.* Evanston: Northwestern UP, 1996.

Lears, Jackson. "A Matter of Taste: Corporate Cultural Hegemony in a Mass-Consumption Society." *Recasting America: Culture and Politics in the Age of Cold War.* Ed. Larry May. Chicago: U of Chicago P, 1989. 38–59.

Levi-Strauss, Claude. *The Raw and the Cooked.* Trans. John and Doreen Weightman. New York: Harper & Row, 1969.

Lewis, J. Patrick. *Doodle Dandies: Poems That Take Shape.* New York: Atheneum Books for Young Readers, 1998.

Livingston, Myra Cohn. *The Child as Poet: Myth or Reality?* Boston: Horn Book,

1984.

———. "David McCord's Poems: Something Behind the Door." *Touchstones: Reflections on the Best in Children's Literature.* Ed. Perry Nodelman. Vol. 2. West Lafayette: ChLA, 1987. 157–72.

———. "The Light in His Attic." *New York Times Book Review.* March 9, 1986: 36.

———. "The Poem on Page 81." *Only Connect: Readings on Children's Literature.* 3rd ed. Ed. Sheila Egoff, et al. Toronto: Oxford UP, 1996. 214–24.

———, ed. *Why Am I Grown So Cold? Poems of the Unknowable.* New York: Atheneum, 1983.

Lodge, Sally. "Children's Poetry in Bloom." *Publishers Weekly.* April 1, 2002 <http://publishersweekly.reviewsnews.com/index.asp?layout'articlePrint&articleID' CA205454>.

Lowell, Robert. *The Letters of Robert Lowell.* Ed. Saskia Hamilton. New York: Farrar, Straus and Giroux, 2005.

———. "Randall Jarrell." *Randall Jarrell, 1914–1965.* Ed. Robert Lowell, Peter Taylor, and Robert Penn Warren. New York: Farrar, Straus and Giroux, 1967. 101–12.

———. *Selected Poems.* Rev. ed. New York: Farrar, Straus and Giroux, 1977.

MacDonald, Ruth. *Shel Silverstein.* New York: Twayne, 1997.

Mariani, Paul. *Lost Puritan: A Life of Robert Lowell.* New York: Norton, 1994.

McClure, John. *Late Imperial Romance.* New York: Verso, 1994.

McGuire, William. *Poetry's Catbird Seat.* Washington, DC: Library of Congress, 1988.

Meyers, Jeffery. *Edmund Wilson: A Biography.* Boston: Houghton Mifflin, 1995.

———. *Robert Frost: A Biography.* Boston: Houghton Mifflin, 1996.

Morgenstern, John. "The Fall into Literacy and the Rise of the Bourgeois Child." *Children's Literature Association Quarterly* 27.3 (2002): 136–45.

Mulvey, Laura. *The Visual and Other Pleasures.* Bloomington: Indiana UP, 1989.

National Poetry Festival: Held in the Library of Congress October 22–24, 1962, Proceedings. Washington, DC: Library of Congress, 1964.

Newcomb, John Timberman. "Canonical Ahistoricism vs. Histories of Canons: Towards Methodological Dissensus." *South Atlantic Review* 54.4 (1989): 3–20.

Niven, Penelope. *Carl Sandburg: A Biography.* New York: Charles Scribner's Sons, 1991.

Nodelman, Perry. "Introduction: Matthew Arnold, a Teddy Bear, and a List of Touchstones." *Touchstones: Reflections on the Best in Children's Literature.* Ed. Perry Nodelman. Vol. 1. West Lafayette: ChLA, 1985. 1–12.

———. *The Pleasures of Children's Literature.* 2nd ed. New York: Longman, 1996.

———. *Touchstones: A List of Distinguished Children's Books.* West Lafayette: ChLA, n.d.

Opie, Iona. *The People in the Playground.* New York: Oxford UP, 1993.

Padgett, Ron. Foreword. *Wishes, Lies, and Dreams: Teaching Children to Write Poetry.* By Kenneth Koch. New York: HarperCollins, 1999. xii–xix.

———. "Nine Years under the Masthead of Teachers and Writers Collaborative." *Journal of a Living Experiment: A Documentary History of the First Ten Years of Teachers and Writers Collaborative.* Ed. Phillip Lopate. New York: Teachers and

Writers, 1979. 282–88.

Parini, Jay. *Robert Frost: A Life*. New York: Henry Holt and Company, 1999.

Perelman, Bob. *Marginalization of Poetry: Language Writing and Literary History*. Princeton, NJ: Princeton UP, 1996.

Perloff, Marjorie. *Radical Artifice: Writing Poetry in the Age of Media*. Chicago: U of Chicago P, 1991.

———, et al. "The Yale *Symphosymposium* on Contemporary Poetics and Concretism: A World View from the 1990s." *Experimental, Visual, Concrete: Avant-Garde Poetry Since the 1960s*. Ed. K. David Jackson, Eric Vos, and Johanna Drucker. Atlanta: Rodopi, 1996. 369–416.

Philip, Neil. "The Shared Moment: Thoughts on Children & Poetry." Rev. of *From the Garden to the Street: An Introduction to 300 Years of Poetry*, by Morag Styles. *Signal* 88 (Jan. 1999): 3–15.

Prelutsky, Jack. *The New Kid on the Block*. New York: Greenwillow, 1984.

———, ed. *The Random House Book of Poetry for Children: A Treasury of 572 Poems for Today's Child*. New York: Random House, 1983.

Pritchard, William H. *Randall Jarrell: A Literary Life*. New York: Farrar, Straus and Giroux, 1990.

Ransom, John C. "Constellation of Five Young Poets." *Critical Essays on Randall Jarrell*. Ed. Suzanne Ferguson. Boston: G. K. Hall, 1983. 15–16.

Rasula, Jed. *American Poetry Wax Museum: Reality Effects, 1940–1990*. Urbana, IL: National Council of Teachers of English, 1995.

Reeves, Richard. *President Kennedy: Profile of Power*. New York: Simon and Schuster, 1993.

Reis, Pedro. "Concrete Poetry: A Generic Perspective." *Experimental, Visual, Concrete: Avant-Garde Poetry Since the 1960s*. Ed. K. David Jackson, Eric Vos, and Johanna Drucker. Atlanta: Rodopi, 1996. 287–302.

Roethke, Theodore. *The Collected Poems of Theodore Roethke*. Garden City, NY: Anchor, 1975.

———. *Dirty Dinky and Other Creatures: Poems for Children by Theodore Roethke*. Garden City, NY: Doubleday, 1973.

———. *I Am! Says the Lamb*. Garden City, NY: Doubleday, 1961.

———. *On the Poet and His Craft: Selected Prose*. Ed. Ralph J. Mills, Jr. Seattle: U of Washington P, 1965.

———. "Open Letter." *Mid-Century American Poets*. Ed. John Ciardi. New York: Twayne, 1950. 67–72.

———. *Party at the Zoo*. New York: Crowell-Collier, 1963.

———. *Selected Letters of Theodore Roethke*. Ed. Ralph J. Mills, Jr. Seattle: U of Washington P, 1968.

———. "Some Remarks on Rhythm." *On Poetry and Craft: Selected Prose of Theodore Roethke*. Port Townsend, WA: Copper Canyon, 2001. 63–74.

———. *Straw for the Fire: From the Notebooks of Theodore Roethke, 1943–1963*. Ed. David Wagoner. Garden City, NY: Doubleday and Co., 1972.

———. "Theodore Roethke Writes . . ." *On Poetry and Craft: Selected Prose of Theodore Roethke*. Port Townsend, WA: Copper Canyon, 2001. 31–33.

———. "Words for Young Writers." *On Poetry and Craft: Selected Prose of Theodore*

Roethke. Port Townsend, WA: Copper Canyon, 2001. 87–97.

Sandburg, Carl. *The American Songbag*. New York: Harcourt, Brace, 1927.

———. *Early Moon*. New York: Harcourt, Brace & World, 1958.

———. *The Letters of Carl Sandburg*. Ed. Herbert Mitgang. New York: Harcourt, Brace & World, 1968.

Seager, Allan. *Glass House: The Life of Theodore Roethke*. New York: McGraw-Hill, 1968.

Shapiro, Harvey. "Rebellious Mythmakers." Rev. of *New American Poetry, 1945–1960*, ed. by Donald M. Allen. *New York Times Book Review*. Aug. 28, 1960: 6.

Shel Silverstein's Adult Works. Feb. 21, 2002 <http://www.banned-width.com/shel. html>.

Sherman, Josepha, and T. K. F. Weisskopf. *Greasy Grimy Gopher Guts: The Subversive Folklore of Childhood*. Little Rock: August House, 1995.

Silverstein, Shel. *Falling Up*. New York: HarperCollins, 1996.

———. *Uncle Shelby's ABZ Book: A Primer for Tender Young Minds*. New York: Simon and Schuster, 1961.

———. *Where the Sidewalk Ends*. New York: HarperCollins, 1974.

Snelson, Karin. Interview with Jack Prelutsky. "Pure Poetry: A Talk with Jack Prelutsky." Feb. 9, 2003. <http://www.amazon.com/exec/obidos/tg/feature/6200/104-1218147-6138305>.

Solt, Mary E. Introduction. "A World Look at Concrete Poetry." *Concrete Poetry: A World View*. Ed. Mary Ellen Solt. Bloomington: Indiana UP, 1970. 6–66.

Spahr, Juliana. *Everybody's Autonomy: Connective Reading and Collective Identity*. Tuscaloosa: U of Alabama P, 2001.

Stephens, John. *Language and Ideology in Children's Fiction*. New York: Longman, 1992.

Styles, Morag. *From the Garden to the Street*. London: Cassell, 1998.

Sutherland, Zena. *Children and Books*. 9th ed. New York: Longman, 1997.

Sword, Elizabeth Hauge, and Victoria McCarthy. *A Child's Anthology of Poetry*. Hopewell, NJ: Ecco, 1995.

Tarr, Anita. "Nonsense Now." *Five Owls* 15.4 (March/April 2001): 85–87.

———. "'Still so much work to be done': Taking up the Challenge of Children's Poetry." Rev. of *From the Garden to the Street: An Introduction to 300 Years of Poetry* by Morag Styles. *Children's Literature* 28 (2000): 195–201.

Thomas, Joseph T., Jr. "Mel Glenn and Arnold Adoff: The Poetics of Power in the Adolescent Voice-lyric." *Style* 35.3 (2001): 486–97.

———. "Reappraising Uncle Shelby." *Horn Book Magazine*. May/June 2005: 283–93.

Townsend, John Rowe. *Written for Children*. 3rd rev. ed. New York: Lippincott, 1987.

Travisano, Thomas. *Midcentury Quartet: Bishop, Lowell, Jarrell, Berryman, and the Making of a Postmodern Aesthetic*. Charlottesville: UP of Virginia, 1999.

———. "Randall Jarrell's Poetics: A Rediscovered Milestone." *Georgia Review* 50.4 (1996): 691–96.

Tyler, Parker. "The Dramatic Lyricism of Randall Jarrell." *Critical Essays on Randall Jarrell*. Ed. Suzanne Ferguson. Boston: G. K. Hall, 1983. 140–48.

Untermeyer, Louis, ed. *The Golden Treasury of Poetry.* New York: Golden, 1959.

Usrey, Malcolm. Forward. *Touchstones: Reflections on the Best in Children's Literature.* Ed. Perry Nodelman. Vol. 2. Gen. West Lafayette: ChLA, 1987. v–vi.

Vendler, Helen. "Ha—mine soul—I say 'alas' and I say 'alas' and 'alas'!" Rev. of Jerome Rothenberg and George Quasha's *America: A Prophecy* (1973) *New York Times Book Review.* Dec. 30, 1973: 7–8.

Vidler, Anthony. *The Architectural Uncanny: Essays in the Modern Unhomely.* Cambridge, MA: MIT P, 1992.

Warren, Robert P. *New and Selected Essays.* New York: Random House, 1989.

———. "Robert Penn Warren." *Poets at Work: The* Paris Review *Interviews.* Ed. George Plimpton. New York: Penguin, 1989. 3–24.

Weinman, Sarah. *The Shel Silverstein Archive.* Feb. 22, 2003 <http://shelsilverstein.tripod.com/>.

Wells, Henry W. "The Poetry of Carl Sandburg." *Voices: A Quarterly of Poetry* 125 (1946): 39–45.

Wilbur, Richard. *Conversations with Richard Wilbur.* Ed. William Butts. Jackson: UP of Mississippi, 1990.

Wildman, Eugene, ed. *An Anthology of Concretism.* Chicago: Swallow, 1969.

Yannella, Philip R. *The Other Carl Sandburg.* Jackson: UP of Mississippi, 1996.

Index

Permissions Acknowledgments

"Mirror" reprinted with the permission of Atheneum Books for Young Readers, an imprint of Simon & Schuster Children's Publishing Division, from *Doodle Dandies* by J. Patrick Lewis, illustrated by Lisa Desimini. Text copyright © 1998 by J. Patrick Lewis. Illustrations copyright © 1998 by Lisa Desimini.

"My Yellow Dog" and "The Apple" from *Love That Dog* by Sharon Creech. Copyright © 1998 by Sharon Creech. Used by permission of HarperCollins Publishers.

DATE DUE

MAR 1 1 2010			

DEMCO 38-296